Mixed-up Blessing

Mixed-up Blessing

A new encounter with being church

Barbara Glasson

British Library Cataloguing in Publication data

A catalogue record for this book is available from the British Library

ISBN 1 85852 305 2

First published by Inspire
4 John Wesley Road
Werrington
Peterborough PE4 6ZP

Printed and bound in Great Britain by
Athenaeum Press Ltd, Gateshead, Tyne & Wear

Contents

Death of a Church, Life of a City

'It's time to put your hand in.'
'What, in there?'
'Yep, in that sludgy mess.'
'Are you sure it's going to be bread, Barbara?'
'Sure I'm sure.'
'I've never made bread before.'
'Tell you what, I'll believe in you and you believe in the bread.'
'In there then?'
'Yep, up to your elbows, right in there.'

This is the story of a new way of being church. This church is called Somewhere Else and it has found its life in the centre of Liverpool. This is a story of encouragement. That is, I hope it will give you courage, whether you are hanging on in there with the church, or fell out of it a long time ago. I hope it will also encourage you even if your life has never crossed paths with any church but you still believe that your spirit has some mysterious connection with God's spirit. This is not a particularly neat story. It has been at times confusing and complex. I could have edited out all the blind alleys and idiosyncrasies, but that would not encourage you. I know that life makes very little sense going forwards yet I want to encourage you to go straight on into the muddle, to take the risk of engaging with your own story with all its wonder and struggle and of hearing echoes of God ahead of you. Then to be prompted to live the possibility of allowing the gospel story to intertwine with all this confusing experience. I intend to encourage you to take a risk and find hints of delight and mystery in your experience.

This is not a story of how we got things right. Somewhere Else is not an ideal church. It does not offer any short cuts to the perfect community. On the contrary, this is a hard story and we are a work in progress. We have some tough struggles and at times this is a truly uncomfortable environment. All of us come with complex experiences and varying levels of tolerance. It takes courage to confront issues. It is not easy to acknowledge that we have limits to our own ability to accept diversity. When we fall out with people it is easier to blame them or ignore what is really happening. There are times when we have got things spectacularly wrong. Much of our experience makes no sense at all. This is how it is. So, the encouragement I want to give is for you to go straight on into your own hard places, not as a retreat from church but a discovery of a new depth of being church where you are. This is where God meets us – face to face in our confusion and mess. At least that is what we are coming to believe at Somewhere Else.

Starting from nowhere

I suppose most journeys begin with a question. 'I wonder what's round the next bend.' 'I wonder where that staircase goes.' 'I wonder if I am in love.' I guess that while we ask questions hoping for an answer we are mostly not rewarded with an instant solution to our wondering but rather some process of discovery unfolds for us. For the intrepid, questions call us forward into new possibilities and more questions. That is the terror and the joy of them.

From an early age, we may have been discouraged to ask questions – or at least questions that have no answers. Yet they are what give us the edge to discovering our lives. Faith is not so much about signing up to a set of certainties but about engaging with the questions that pester our peace of mind. It may not be the purpose of a question that it receives an instant answer, rather that we learn to live with the question, revisiting why it niggles us and letting it disturb us sufficiently to keep on working with it. The question I was given five years ago was, 'Is there a place for the Methodist church in Liverpool city centre?' This is not your question. Only you know what your question is and it will start you from a different place from mine. Creativity emerges when we live courageously with the question that is given particularly to us.

People have asked me subsequently if I ever had a job description. The answer is 'yes' and this is it. 'Go and find if there's a place for the Methodist church in the city centre, Barbara, and for God's sake do something different.' That was how I found myself driving the car having a word with God. It went something like this: 'Help! This is a very, very large city and I am only five foot two inches high, I haven't got the first idea what I'm supposed to be doing and I do not know where to start. So you'd better be there or we're all sunk!' I have never found God to be very good on answering emergency prayers directly – in my experience he tends to get round to it eventually somewhere down the line. But on this occasion a word came straight into my head. The word was 'bread'. It seemed a ridiculous enough concept to have some possibilities. So, on 1 September 1999, I took the train into Liverpool city centre convinced of only two things. First, I was intended to be there and second, it had something to do with bread.

Some days later I came to be sitting under the statue of the Moores brothers outside Littlewoods. The statue depicts the brothers deep in conversation, walking up Church Street. Even in their bronze form they seem so familiar with the city, confident about their surroundings. They belong to this place, and by contrast I was feeling very lost. Streets that others referred to easily by name were still grid references in my rather dog-eared *A–Z*. If I asked for directions I would still get serious suggestions like 'Turn right where the cinema used to be'. On top of this, those familiar points of reference that conventionally give ministers their bearing were not available to me – like a church building or a congregation. The Methodist Central Hall had closed some years before after a long history of social action and eloquent preaching. It had been the gathering point for many younger people who had escaped local congregations to socialize there as well as be inspired by the popular preachers of the day. A congregation that had dwindled to 14 members reluctantly, and with a great deal of pain, had finally shut the door on the premises. The building still occupies one side of Renshaw Street but is now operating as a casino and nightclub. I can only speculate at the sense of defeat that small congregation must have felt. At this time they must have felt lost too.

Not having a building has some advantages as long as you have good shoes. If you do not have a door then you cannot close it. Sitting under the statue caused me to begin to listen to what was going on around me. There were two shop assistants having a smoke on the doorstep while having a gripe about a colleague. There was a mother pushing a buggy with a screaming child. Next to me an old bloke was eating some sandwiches. There was a whole tide of people flowing in and out of doorways, trying to avoid bumping into each other in the street. When it rained I adjourned to a café. While pretending to write things in my diary, I eavesdropped on conversations and noticed who was around. I saw any number of grannies with young children, people meeting friends in lunch hours, quite a large number of men in casual clothes. As the days went by I began to notice more and more. To look up above the shopfronts and admire architecture obscured by modern signs at street level. Trees that grew out of roofs, a persistent blackbird serenading from a chimney stack, the incessant circling of gulls and hopeful pigeons.

I also began to notice a rhythm to the day. Sometimes, arriving in the early morning, I met the first tide of people approaching the city centre's common ground. Cleaners, road sweepers and a few drunks left over from the night before brought the city into life in readiness for the next wave of smartly dressed shop and office workers. The first cheap train of the day brought in the babies and pensioners. *Big Issue* guys appeared, depending on what day of the week it was – never around on Thursdays, that being benefit day. I got talking with Leo who sold the *Issue* at the bottom of Bold Street – he spoke four different languages – and Tony from Glasgow soon started to look out for me. In Lewis's I discovered the remarkable ministry of the 'women in wigs' and visited the pensioners' tea party in BHS.

There was a lull in proceedings at around seven o'clock in the evening – as if it was a moment for the city to take a breath before the influx of younger people who would dance and shout their way into the early hours. Contact with the police revealed that this was so well orchestrated that this central area was, despite the occasional shooting, far safer than the suburbs at night. It was in this way that I discovered the city as a living place – it has a heartbeat and a pulse, there is a rhythm to the day, with high and low tides.

So, as I wandered in the city centre I discovered that the city is an organic reality – it breathes and rests, washes and dances, struggles and is wounded.

It has a life that is rich and complex and diverse. And it also has people. As the weeks went by I began to be less lost. Leo would engage me in conversation. Side by side at the bottom of Bold Street I not only got to know some of his story but also how it feels to stand as people push past him as if he was invisible. His 'regulars' would bring him chocolate bars or cans of Coke but others deliberately gave him a wide berth or would call him names or spit.

Meanwhile, the 'women in wigs' had a whole thing going in the corner of Lewis's. With a great deal of good humour and kindness, mixed with considerable skill at selling, they talked people through their new image, their sexuality or their battle against cancer. Customers not only bought things but also felt better about themselves, they put their fears to one side for a bit and laughed themselves into a different place.

September turned into October. Christmas was everywhere. I noticed a tree appear in Lewis's with tags tied on with ribbons. Closer inspection revealed that it was possible to make a donation to a local hospice and buy a tag to decorate the tree. Anyone could write something on a tag – the name of somebody they wanted to remember or a situation that was worrying them. As the weeks went by the tree acquired more and more tags. It stood out among all the plastic Christmas hype as a sign of something different going on.

This rich but confusing encounter pushed me into new questions about myself and this place. If God was ahead of me as I had hoped, where was he and how could I recognize where the spirit was at work? People were not unkind as I wandered around wearing a clerical collar, although some took pains to avoid me, but what if anything did I have to say here? What is good news? I was in the process of un-learning a great many things. T.S. Eliot wrote in his

Four Quartets, 'We can have the experience but miss the meaning'. It was soon apparent that there was some thinking needed around this experience. It was beginning to challenge some of my assumptions about ministry. I became aware that I had less to bring and more to learn. This wandering also began to challenge the way I felt about myself. How could I be an authentic minister to Leo or to the 'women in wigs'? They had their own way of being, their own stories, their own experiences. The whole concept of 'church' felt a million miles away.

There was a nagging sense of doubt in myself – was this real ministry when there were churches without ministers? Had I studied theology for four years to go wandering around shops all day? I had to fend off quite a deal of skitting from fellow ministers – even at home. One of my sons, faced with the question in his German oral exam, 'What does your mother do for a living?' had replied, 'She gives out leaflets in the city'! Where was God in this entire muddle? If God was ahead of me as I had supposed, how could I know? Where was the God who sustained my faith and internal sense of being? There was a lot of shifting sand, a lot of nonsense.

So, rather than looking for instant answers I encourage you also to begin to live out your nonsense. Not just in a mental way of going round and round at the same thing, but a physical engagement with the things that make no sense at all. Living with the nonsense of things is the beginning of a creative encounter. The first encounters I experienced were with the geography and physicality of the city centre. This experience was earthed, on the ground, under my feet. In this way I began to get a sense of place.

A sense of place

How do we understand the place where we live? I happen to work in a city centre, but all places have identities. These identities change, through history, through the seasons of the year, even within the same day. If we believe God is ahead of us then we need to have courage to explore our surroundings. We may never have looked at it before. Certainly most of us go around with things on our minds distracting us from our environment. If we go to a Methodist church the stewards probably lock the door during the first hymn. The physical, vibrant, earthed place we find ourselves in is the context in which we are called to discover what God is about. Incarnation is about a God in the here and now, up to something. If we do not go around with our eyes open then how will we perceive the layers of that divine presence or the wonder and struggle of the people?

The population of Liverpool is in the order of 500,000. Across the water, on a curious peninsula between the Mersey and the Dee, lies the mysterious land of Wirral. Connecting these worlds a link of trains and ferries focuses on the city centre. Liverpool is marinated in history; it has soaked into its bones and architecture. The crypt at St Anthony's Roman Catholic Church witnesses to the many, including seven local priests, who died during the worst of the Irish Potato Famine. The Irish brought with them, among other gifts, their tenacity to Roman Catholic faith and culture. Half the patients signing in at local hospitals still describe themselves as Roman Catholic. Two cathedrals witness to days of sectarianism in a time gallantly breached by dialogue and friendships.

Theatres and art galleries demonstrate the curious wit of the place. Welsh and Irish histories mix to give a lyricism and humour. Generations of poverty add to the mix — tough women who have survived beleaguered times speak their minds. There are stories to tell. Similarly there are signs of ages long gone – shipping lines and slave ships that gave the city some of its finest architecture and some of its cause for sorrow that prosperity often comes at the expense of the fortunes of others. Tales of grievances born out of unkept promises, regeneration that failed to take root, sharpness to the edge of the tongue. Yet, underneath, a wicked sense of fun that simply bubbles to the surface. I was reminded of this on a recent easyJet flight home from Dublin, when a certain wit in front of me asked the stewardess, 'This is the Manchester flight, isn't it?' and everyone on the plane dissolved at the sight of the attendant's panic!

And it is a musical place. From the Liverpool Philharmonic to the young musicians at the Zanzibar on a Friday night there is a vibrancy and creativity that focuses on the city centre. It can be belligerent and hot-headed but mostly it is good-natured and talkative.

City centres are the focus of much of this mixture of urban life. They are the neutral spot – everyone's territory. Different cultures or groupings will come and stake their claim in different areas at different times of the day or night on different days of the week. Because of this there are extremes here. Maybe the most marked of all these dichotomies is the cohabitation of extreme prosperity with extreme poverty. International banking and multinational corporations shift millions of pounds around the globe while literally on their doorstep the homeless guys beg enough money for a bed for the night.

Alongside this, Liverpool city centre sees a tide of people returning to live here, an ironic development as planners and bombing had once shifted swathes of population out of town to new developments in Skelmersdale and Kirkby. Now city centre dwelling is fashionable and penthouse flats sell for up to a million pounds. These dwellings are often in gated apartment blocks, second homes that are vacated at weekends as workers return to families elsewhere.

Liverpool also has three universities, all with city centre sites. This increases the population of the city significantly in term time as full-time students take up residence, and that is in addition to those studying part-time in colleges. Student populations bring vibrancy to the life of the city centre, accompanied by aspects of loneliness and displacement.

Asylum seekers arrange to meet in St John's Market where it is dry and goods are cheaper than most. People seeking work flock to the city centre Jobcentres and agencies. Others looking for anonymity come in for support groups and counselling. Tourists arrive for the 'Liverpool Experience' and splash into the Albert Dock on a big yellow duck. All of us walk on the same pavement. It is the gift and challenge of the city centre.

I can wager that you have probably heard a joke about Liverpool that mentions missing wheels. Even among local people there is a fear of bringing cars into the city centre at night. Insurance premiums are higher here – which is one reason why the people of Wirral wanted to hang on to their Cheshire postcode. If there is a rogue in a TV drama, chances are they'll have something like a Scouse accent (usually a pretty poor imitation). Often, when I am at a meeting away from the city people will ask the customary, 'Where do you come from?' When I respond 'Liverpool', there is often a pause followed by, 'You don't sound as if you do,' which I take to mean that I do not fit the stereotype. Liverpool has weathered years of prejudice yet the city centre has more Georgian buildings than any other English town outside Bath. It was nominated for World status as a heritage city and the successful City of Culture bid brought a cheer on the Merseyrail link when the guard announced it one morning over the intercom. The Merseyside police have been pioneers in community policing and the city centre is managed with a keen eye to the safety of those who come for recreation.

There are perceived jealousies between Liverpool and Manchester, as Liverpool has sensed it has been sidelined in favour of the larger city. The development of Liverpool John Lennon Airport has brought new life beyond such jealousies but they run deep and are often most readily observed in the tribalism associated with football teams.

I have had to learn all this. Although I have, now, lived in Liverpool longer than I have lived anywhere else, I will always be a stranger here. I do not have the blood of the place flowing in my veins. I have the eye of an outsider that can sometimes see what a local does not perceive. So, I walked and talked and listened and learned to wait. I was beginning to live the lost-ness of things. I was struggling to live without many of the familiar signposts of church and I sensed the deepest loneliness. Living out our own loneliness is a tough agenda, yet to ignore it is like always paddling in the shallow end. Jumping into the context of the questions with which we live means that we are often on a solitary journey. Maybe only in our loneliness can we sense the depth of the greater mystery of which our own questions form a small part.

Being lost

Loneliness comes from many sources and it is not necessarily about being alone. I knew that part of the calling to be in the city centre was not to fall too easily into anybody else's agenda. It was open season to invite me on to committees! I succumbed to a few but on the whole tried to resist being pulled in. That was hard, because it is much more immediately satisfying to be sucked into 'doing something' than living out the lonely process of 'just being there'. 'What exactly is it you are doing in the city?' people would ask. It was enough to push all my buttons about 'earning my living' and 'being of use'. Waiting and watching, listening and learning are not to be hurried and I knew I had to be patient with the process, but it was difficult to explain to people who were used to living with tasks and goals. 'This is Barbara, she walks the streets', was the usual jibe, followed by rather suggestive laughter. I tried to take it in good part, but what was this about really? The whole process colluded with my insecurities.

'What's up, Barbara?' Leo asked one day as I had had a particular fraught time in Tesco Metro. I tried to explain. 'Don't you worry,' he said as I left to go home, 'I'll watch out for you.'

It was nearly Christmas. The run-up had been mind-bending. The manager of BHS explained how the displays were organized to meet the trends in people's shopping. 'First we put out the kids' stuff, then it's the slippers and nighties, and the week before Christmas it's the women's gifts – everyone leaves them until last.' I began to realize the competitive and ruthless way the market was being managed. How the psyche of shopping was being manipulated – people will always make sure the kids have something – and how the staff were working long hours in the Christmas shop. They would be in again all night the day after Boxing Day to set out the sale goods. It seemed relentless. Despite participating in endless carol services at the parish church I seemed to have lost sight of where God is incarnate in all this. Christmas Eve came, the city went quiet and I went home.

I had been a minister in a suburban church for the last five years. Christmas was a season when there was plenty to do, services to organize, people to visit in hospital, excitement to share with children. That first Christmas in the city took all that away from me. I began to realize that God comes into the world silently and unannounced. It was not in my power to make him arrive. In the scenario of office parties and carol services and frantic shopping I felt robbed of any way of proclaiming what I saw as the reality of Christmas – Christ with us, making a difference to the poor and rejected. The whole swathe of commercial scheming and prosperous assumptions was cutting through any thought of doing it differently. I had no voice, no impact and no influence. I was tired and cold. My shoes were getting holes in them and I was totally confused. Was I just wandering around for nothing? Who noticed if I was there or not anyway? Was it all senseless? Maybe I should just call it a day and get home.

Leo was complaining of having no heating in his place. The boiler had packed up and the landlord could not do anything about it until after the festive season. We had an old electric heater in the garage so we took it round to his flat which we eventually located on the outskirts of town. It was indeed freezing, very sparsely furnished and there was another occupant sleeping on the settee. Leo offered us a drink which we accepted and left. Days on the street, nights in the cold, addictions, fears, disassociation and terrors were all the fabric of his daily existence. Christmas loomed at him, a whole week without selling the *Issue*, without a reason to get up in the morning. Yet Leo had said, 'I'll watch out for you, Barbara.' It has always struck me as curious that it is the people with the least who will offer you the most.

Watching and waiting

Whatever the context of our questioning, it is important that we watch and wait. It is easy to jump quickly into a set of solutions because they help us come to closure on the hard process of living our questions. If we close down we exclude. Living with possibilities is hard. There are so many strands to experience that when they remain unresolved we are left feeling unsatisfied. For me those early months were about observing, watching and waiting. It was very challenging. It would have been much easier to plant a church, start a community project or even preach in the streets. Now, five years on from those early wanderings, I see that they were the most important part of the whole process. I had no option but to let the city speak its own story. If I wanted to get to understand and love this place there was no other way than to listen to it speaking to me. Some of the things I encountered challenged me to the centre of my being. Why was there always someone asking me for money? Why did parents take their screaming babies shopping? Why do people conduct their arguments on the streets on their mobile phones when they could have left them at home? Other things delighted me. I began to appreciate the design and balance of buildings, to see the breaking in of the natural world through cracks in the pavement, to see how people worked well.

I also started to appreciate that the city has its own character and life. That it is a free, living organism that could be both healthy and pathological. I acknowledged the privilege of being able to observe what was going on. Who else was there, present to the moods and tensions of the city in this way without a pre-set agenda for change? On bad days the experience was quite overwhelming, there seemed little hope that there was a way into all of this. I was tired and confused. At other times, and usually quite out of the blue, came exquisite moments of surprise. They were often from the most unexpected places.

Over the weeks I began to see the turnaround in what was happening both inside me and around me. I was breaking free from those patterns of power in which I assumed I was going to be the one to bring something to the place. Instead I saw the place as a gift that would offer up its own insights and connections. I needed to be perceptive enough to recognize this when it happened. I began to see that 'ministry' wasn't my offering to Liverpool, rather that I was in a place to recognize and affirm the ministry that was already going on here – the ministry of Leo and the 'women in wigs', of Tony the master salesman of the *Big Issue* who watched out for his customers, and all those who believed in each other and in this place. It began to dawn on me how enormous and tiny God is.

Alongside these wandering days there were days in Sheila's kitchen. I had already shared with some of my closest friends the idea of the bread. There are times when you have to hand it to your closest friends. Despite the fact that this was clearly crazy they went along with it and we met one morning armed with yeast and bags of flour in Sheila's kitchen.

'So how do we make bread, then?' someone asked, looking expectantly in my direction. I'm no cook, in fact somewhere in my school career I had given up cookery in favour of Latin, but I had made bread with my children when we had been looking for something creative to do on a dull day. 'Well, I only know how to do it with 3 pounds of flour at a time ... 9 spoons of yeast, a pint and a half of warm water, I use honey not sugar ...'

Initial trepidation soon dispersed into a rather riotous morning, up to our elbows in stickiness. As the dough was left to rise by the fire we drank coffee and laughed. 'I remember making bread with my granny years ago', someone remembered. Stories began to flow. By lunchtime the bread was in the oven and we sat to eat. The conversation had hit a deeper spot. We were sharing some concerns about our children. A couple of us had houses full of young adults with all the challenges that presented. It was good to have time to talk about our struggles with temperaments and space.

By the middle of the afternoon there was bread everywhere. We had all made three loaves and we were feeling rather proud of ourselves. It smelled gorgeous. 'What are we going to do with all this?' We agreed that we would take one loaf home for the people who lived in our house – it promised a good reception when we walked through the door bearing hot bread. The other loaves we chose to give away. At first it was difficult to know who we would give it to, but gradually each of us had an idea. 'I'm going to take it to the woman next door, I haven't seen her for ages.' 'I'm going to take it to my mum, we need to make peace!' 'I'm going to take it to Bill because Joan's in hospital and he's feeling sorry for himself.' So it went on. We wrapped the loaves like newly born babies and set off with our gifts.

Inner space and outer space

As the weeks flowed into each other a rhythm began to develop. It wasn't the usual pattern of the working week – indeed my week was all over the place – but there was a pace of engagement and withdrawal that was initiated by the bread. Bread-making became my point of connection to a different set of people. This group was never the same group twice. As the bread was made and distributed, so others were intrigued by what was going on. 'Why did you make this for me? Did you say anyone could come?' In the same way as the city began to reveal a life of its own, so also the bread-making began to have life. We found that we looked forward to those days set aside to gather around Sheila's kitchen table. One of the gifts of making bread is that it takes time and cannot be rushed. In the waiting and watching with the dough we had space for laughter and stories.

I had lost the sense of seasonality in the city centre as Christmas merged into Easter. We began to discover another seasonality – it was the bread that gave pace and order to the days. It was a different sort of encounter that began to make the connection between what was happening 'out there' in the external, physical, frenetic world of the city and what was happening 'in here' in the very deepest parts of my being.

At the time I wrote:

> *This is not an empty space. The city is occupied by Christmas shoppers, office workers, homeless men, women and children and by noise. Neither is it devoid of churches, although many have left. This is a full-up place, full of busy-ness and business, commerce, retail and destitution. Roofless warehouses, topless women, thoughtless executives, wealth and poverty in all its fullness.*
>
> *And it is occupied by ghosts.*
>
> *Gladstone still walks along Rodney Street, bag in hand, with the reverie of the philanthropist. Newton, the slave ship owner turned priest can be heard to hum the tune of 'Amazing Grace' along*

the back jigger of Rope Walks. The macabre freedom songs of human cargoes, tied up with the frayed ropes of ideologies, moor at the Albert Dock. And everywhere there are crowds of nostalgia for overhead railways, for tall-masted ships, for communities displaced by bombs, for the Cavern and youth and for the many times that Liverpool has been great.

Other ghosts too. Ghosts of potato famines and thousands of migrant children dying in the workhouse and the Toxteth riots and Derek Hatton. Spectres of regeneration projects that came and went.

So, to be here, in the city is about place. About here and now and ghosts and memories and aspirations and about pain. Pain of struggling to become something else, something better, something real.

The discovery of space needs to engage with all of this outwardly and inwardly because the space on the outside needs the solidarity of the space on the inside. The soul and the city are required to meet. This encounter is a personal liaison, which involves the vulnerability and intensity of a holy love affair.

The possibility of clearing room for such an encounter starts in the discipline of openness. Opening doors in the stores, in the offices, in the religious institutions. And the opening of doors in

the outer spaces results in the opening of
doors in the inner spaces of memories,
experiences, uncertainties, bereave-
ments, terrors. *The journey into the city
becomes the journey into the soul. It is
an invitation to pain and immense
delight. That is part of what it means to
be here.*

To engage with such self-emptying
may be a frightening experience,
especially for those of us who have
struggled to claim an identity within a
church that we sense has not allowed us
to speak the reality of who we are. Such
a quest has often led to strategies of
assertiveness and defiance. So it
is a risky business to make room
for something else. All might be lost.
Certainly there have been times of
asking, 'What in heaven's name am I
doing here?' and 'What on earth am I
becoming?'

Making space isn't about losing our
identity and personality but about
finding who we are in the depth of our
being and in connection with others. As
in the humbling, emptying and dying of
Jesus we are offered life in all its
fullness. Clearing space, despite its self-
negating prospect, allows the true
flourishing of personhood within
relationships. Given space, people can
claim the possibilities of an identity in
context and with unlikely companions.

So, the transfiguration of the place
and of the person happens because the
city is introduced to the soul and the soul

> *to the city. This relationship is about seeing both with fresh eyes and being able to journey outward and inward – and finding the destination to be the same.'*

Looking back now it seems amazing that I could write in this way so soon after embarking on the process. I suspect that at the time it was more about survival than theology. The rhythm of coming and going into the city centre space, the impact of such intense encounter on me, the need to go away and think about it, the gathering of the bread-makers and the struggle to believe in things as yet unseen, were all hugely demanding. I remember the relief when talking to an experienced city centre minister in Leeds and his words: 'Of course it doesn't make any sense!' There seemed as if nothing remained unchallenged. How did I pray here? Did it make any difference to be ordained? What about sacraments? What was the point of being a Christian when other people were doing such good things? Would I always be a stranger here? Will I always be lost?

On Good Friday I joined the walk of witness through the city centre. A very small group of people gathered at the bombed-out church, St Luke's, at the top of Bold Street. The city shops were buzzing with life. The old guy with the teddy bear head danced his puppets on strings to some electronic music. Someone spat at us. How is it possible to be authentic church in the face of indifference and hatred? How do we un-live some of our oppressive and sectarian heritage? Did I want to be associated with all this? On Good Friday night Leo went back to his flat to shut himself in for a week to face his addiction. I went home. Easter Sunday was a non-event.

So the days unfolded one after the other. Most days I took the train to town, other days were spent in Sheila's kitchen, sometimes I took time elsewhere to talk and think. I endeavoured not to be flattered into taking commitments or be consumed by too much guilt. I began to learn to be present to the city and to discover some of the nuances and contradictions that it revealed. I came to understand that God had called me into being rather than doing, and that being is sometimes a more difficult job than doing and is an authentic way to approach ministry. I listened to the body language of the city as the days and nights took shape, as the tides of people ebbed and flowed. I tried to be present to the people I encountered – to notice when the regular *Big Issue* guys were missing. I struggled to remember names. And I sought to engage with a reflective process that came out of this subjective experience, to value not only what I thought but also how it made me feel. I said my prayers on the train coming in (nobody notices if you've got your eyes shut!) and I tried to be real about my own energy levels. Being and waiting is hard, tiring work.

People asked me, 'Do you have a church yet?' My reply was more defensive than theological: 'Yes, you just can't see it yet!' Going on believing that God is just ahead of us, present yet fleeting, is the challenge of faith. Church helps us to pretend that we have God where we can contain him, where he can be predicted and managed. I think this is a false reality. God is both bigger and smaller than we can ever imagine and infinitely elusive. Our world is full of paradox: what may appear wholesome may in fact be destructive, what seems life-giving can also undermine our freedom. The city seems to act as a magnifying glass to all these puzzles as human experience becomes condensed. We need not only sight but insight to venture into such a context, a depth of field that helps us to perceive the nuance of our humanity. So I tried not to reach firm conclusions but to allow these contradictions to stand alongside each other and to let the space open up rather than to seek to close it down. This is hard.

The summer approached and with it an invitation. I had met Jill at an emergency meeting at the World Shop, the only shop in town that had a good supply of Fairtrade goods. They had been threatened with a trebling of their rent. Their absent landlord had sensed there was an upturn in the fortunes of Bold Street since regeneration was moving up the hill. The World Shop committee pulled in anyone they felt might be able to support them in lobbying for a fairer deal. Jill was at the meeting and so were Linda and myself (Linda was working at that time as a minister in Halewood and was giving the city centre some dedicated time). Jill was noticeable not just because she had a tiny baby attached to her with a length of colourful cloth but because she spoke with confidence and conviction. She offered the World Shop some temporary storage space above the bookshop where she worked. The bookshop is run by a women's cooperative and is called News from Nowhere. After the meeting we fell into conversation and we told her about the bread. Jill invited us to come and look at the rooms, which were, after all, not suitable for the World Shop as they were on the second floor. We went to look because intuition told us that contact with Jill was going to be special.

Providence

Looking back, I can see an amazing Providence in those early days. Maybe it is only ever in looking back that we see the work of Providence. Providence is not about understanding that God is somehow manipulating things to make sure of a certain outcome but rather a conviction that somehow we are accompanied by God within our nonsense and our muddle. The more questions we have, the more we will receive. Questions are a perplexing gift. I was beginning to receive questions about place, poverty and identity. They continue to be areas where I continually struggle with myself in the light of my faith.

Living with questions in relation to a place brought questions about holy ground. Is the city in fact a holy place where God is ahead of us? There are times when it feels far away from anything holy. It can be noisy, offensive and profane. Sometimes it feels like a wilderness. I have been more profoundly lonely here than ever before. I have lost touch with any sense of belonging and wondered whether there is any place where I will ever feel at home.

When the people of Israel were stranded in Egypt, living as slaves among strangers, how did they hold on to a belief that God was ahead of them? It was Moses, standing in front of a burning bush, who was told to take off his shoes because 'the ground on which you stand is holy ground'. Moses was a reluctant hero, not least because he proceeded to take his people into a wilderness where things apparently got a whole lot worse. Despite their persistent grumbling, God provided bread each day, just enough for their needs and double portions at the weekend.

When Moses stood in front of that bush what was it that made that strange ground holy? It was not so much that the earth somehow became a place of sanctity in that particular spot – in many ways the whole earth has been declared holy and no part can claim special favours – but rather it became holy ground for Moses because of his encounter with the God who met him there.

When I set off believing that God was somehow mysteriously ahead of me (and I am not in any other way comparing myself to Moses!) there was a truth that became apparent through encounter – encounter with the physical presence of the city, encounter with my own interior and external wilderness, encounter with other people in all their diversity and wonder.

Jesus' appreciation of the holiness of such an everyday thing as bread came out of his own experience. Maybe most poignantly, out of his wilderness experience where the temptation was to cheat the hunger and the loneliness by turning stones into bread. Jesus knew that, even for the Son of God, wilderness was wilderness. Our sense of desolation and abandonment can promote a terrible sense of God's absence. It is essentially part of the journey of faith but that does not make it any easier. Anyone who can unhesitatingly answer all the questions we ask about God with a string of certainties is a liar. There is always struggle and doubt if we are to grow into new places of understanding. Jesus knew about that when he broke the bread and gave it to that mixed up bunch of followers who were already struggling to hold it together. He even gave bread to Judas. I had looked to bread as a way of connecting with people, a focus around which a community could gather. Now I see that Jesus, faced with the same dilemma, at a point where his physical presence was about to die, had set a precedent for this bread-making community. 'How will you know I am with you when you can't see me?' Jesus asked that early gospel community, and then gave the answer as he held the bread and broke it: 'Here I am.'

In some senses a city centre couldn't be further removed from a wilderness – it is noisy and occupied whereas a wilderness is silent and empty. On the other hand, both can be places of intense loneliness, of isolation, abandonment, self-questioning and temptation. Just as Jesus was tempted to do something spectacular to draw attention to his cause or to gain power and political clout, so I can easily try to take a short cut to the kingdom. But there is authenticity in being present in a harsh environment and letting the challenges and threats of a place impact our way of being. In some ways it was easy for me, I had permission to wait and wonder. For those whose daily living is earned in commerce or retail or who spend their lives waiting on street corners, the wilderness of the city is raw and harsh. Yet there is solidarity in being there that strikes deeper than words. Jesus simply put his body where his faith was and I guess we are called to do the same. Standing alongside the vulnerable and dispossessed isn't an armchair mental exercise, it is about being physically present to a place and its people. It is dangerous, costly and bewildering.

There is a gospel imperative to engage with the poor, but who are the poor? I am tempted to say that it's the homeless guys who drift in and out of the city, the asylum seekers and the young men who sleep where they can and get fixes how they can. There is, of course, truth here, but poverty is more than this. As a society we are all responsible for those who fall through the net of provision. No one chooses to live on the streets if there is a safer option, but often 'home' is not a safe place and addictions drive people to desperation. There is also another order of homeless people who, while having prosperous jobs and material assets, are rootless and lonely. Working late and losing a sense of connection with families or friends, their lives can become disjointed and impoverished. Poverty is less about who is prosperous and more about who is generous. I sense that it is those who are generous who are rich and those who are hard-minded and critical who are the poor both in the gospel story and in our Liverpool story.

Here is an example. I was trying to deliver some pots and pans to our building in Bold Street. They had been given to me by a local Boots store and were in the back of my car. Parking was tight and I had stopped opposite the door and a little up the street, hoping a traffic warden wouldn't materialize. This proved to be a logistical problem because I was going to have to make several trips – I had to get the boxes out of the boot of my car, close the boot and lock the car, cross the street, open the door with a big bunch of keys and put the pans inside. It was getting very complicated with the keys. There was a guy in a doorway selling the *Big Issue* and I went to ask him if he would mind putting his foot in the doorway while I went backwards and forwards to the car. 'No worries, love,' he said, 'I'll get the boxes for you.' Without another word I was left holding the door while he went to and fro ferrying the pans from the car. I confess to my shame that I was worried in case he made off with the boxes or pinched something out of the car. Afterwards I thanked him – he had made a tricky job manageable and I was honestly very grateful. 'It's OK, love,' he said, 'you just can't be too careful these days, you don't know who's around.'

Now, who in this story is poor?

So, the path of Providence is a path of nonsense and challenge that leaves no stone unturned. If I encourage you to embark on a path of being church in a new way then this is what is in store for you. There may be a day in which you can look back and see the hand of Providence in your journey. You may never see it. You may just experience great tides of questions that at times may seem overwhelming. Every certainty will become doubted, you may lose what you had thought to be your faith. It is a risk.

Working out what it means

The theologian Jürgen Moltmann worked with the sense of God's abandonment in the face of the Holocaust. It was an attempt to make sense of the destructiveness of war and still believe in a God of love. This struggle has continued in recent decades as we endeavour to see evidence of God's activity in the context of a postmodern world where society sometimes struggles to find some cohesion and mostly lives without it. Two polarized temptations emerge for the religious, the first to cling to religious fundamentalism where questions can be answered by certainties, the second to abandon religion with preference for individual lifestyle choices. Falling between the two, the moderate churches have seemingly lost their voices. They have in effect been silenced or rubbished as having nothing worth saying. I suggest that we are called to stand firmly within this silence and listen to what is being said to us by this apparently absent God. There is a calling to look at places 'as though he had looked at them too' and to stand there long enough to catch a glimpse of the reflection.

The city centre experience quickly taught me that this 'standing in the spaces' is not a soft option. To be authentic to the rich diversity of human experience takes us to the very edges of our own understanding. There are no certainties except that we are required to stand, watch, listen and pray.

I suggest that the beginning of catching sight of a reflection of God's presence depends on the value we place on our own experience. People will often say to me by way of apology, 'I'm not religious,' by which they usually mean they do not subscribe to a set of doctrines or rules that they perceive are the requirements of faith. The same people will talk intelligently about their lives and experiences and ask deep and profound questions about what it all means.

Rosemary Radford Ruether writes:

> Experience is the starting point and the ending point of the hermeneutical circle. Codified tradition both reaches back to roots in experience and is constantly renewed or discarded through the test of experience. 'Experience' includes experience of the divine, experience of oneself and experience of the community and the world in an interacting dialectic. (Ruether, 1983, p. 12)

Dialectic is a conversation that brings all the areas of our lives to talk with each other. Usually theologians talk of dialectic between tradition, experience, Scripture and reason and different strands of theology give different points of embarkation. I want to encourage you to begin with experience, because it is the place where everyone can get in on the conversation. We all have experiences so we can all talk. Then there is the need to hold the Scriptures and tradition alongside the experiences, not to correct them or interpret them in a set way but rather so that they can shed light upon each other. So, it seems that the courage to live our nonsense is initially a process of watching, waiting, listening and reflecting. We need to go on believing in this elusive God who walks in front of us yet is so hard to perceive. In all this there is a need to engage with our own loneliness, the depth of solitude in which God is a constant if sometimes elusive companion. In the deep silences at the heart of our own isolation we come to a connection between the spirit of the place, our own spirit and the spirit of the one who is greater than both. Who we are and where we find ourselves is our gift. In this engagement we need good friends and wise counsellors. We may be lonely but we should not be isolated. The courage to take on this life-giving journey is the starting point for what will unfold. In this we need to trust the Spirit, who will most definitely bring some surprises – as we were about to find out!

Surprising companions

One of the many gifts that have come to the Somewhere Else community has been unexpected and surprising people. Some have been co-opted but others have just turned up from all over the place. This is now a place with a life of its own and we are all learning to speak out of our experience and give our own views and insights. So, while I begin this story with my own journey of discovery, you will hear other voices beginning to emerge as the tale unfolds. Rather than me doing all the talking, it is much more appropriate that the people of the place should begin to speak for themselves, so you will hear voices other than mine. You will realize that we are a bunch of extraordinarily ordinary people, each a living part of this narrative.

Linda writes:

> *A year of meeting together, of Barbara trudging the streets, meeting people and listening, of making bread in borrowed kitchens, gathering strangers together around the kneading and rising, of listening out for where the life and energy is, of recognizing our need of a place for now, for baking bread. Then, after all this waiting, at a chaotic meeting about the fragile future of the Liverpool World Shop, we hear of a vacant flat to rent above News from*

Nowhere, a radical bookshop run and owned by a women's cooperative.

It takes a long time, but eventually we take on the lease to 'Somewhere Else'. I mean, what else can you call church in a flat above News from Nowhere?

We took on the lease, but how to be church? Various groups already met in the flat and they were to continue to do so: Falun Gong, STEPS – a self-help group for women who self harm – and RASA, a counselling service for women who have been raped or sexually abused. So was it their space, or News from Nowhere's or ours? We were joining other people in a space that was already theirs, where they gathered to share some of the most fragile and important aspects of their lives. They were welcoming us, and showing us how to be human, real, vulnerable.

The women from News from Nowhere welcomed us unconditionally. They trusted us to be real, honest, have needs and things to share. They were non-judgemental about who we were, when they had every ground for being suspicious of church as being excluding, judging, moralistic, unaffirming of what they held most dear. They were clear about their own criteria for groups to use the building and their right of veto.

I wondered how it would have been if the tables were turned, as they more often are, if the church owned the building and was letting a part out to a bookshop or a room to a group. Would we have been so unconditional or non-judgemental or generous? Would we have interrogated them based on our suspicions? Would we have understood that the space was truly shared, not ours to control, that all people have equal worth and a right to a safe space to be?

It seemed that power was being used differently here. We weren't in control, setting the ground rules alone or able to enjoy the power-good feeling that comes with being able to let out our space magnanimously. There is power, of course, power held more equally by everyone rather than the few, power which empowers, protects. It is a power up from the people, the roots, diverse, shared, not down from a controlling centre.

Everyone else was showing us how to be church. It is simply there in the connectedness between human beings seeking to be faithful to the whole of their experience, their body, the world, their hurt and their wholeness, their power to act in the world, a way of being. It is there in the trust placed in each other as valued human beings and in the sort of unconditional welcome which flows from that. It was there in the need of us all for a safe space to be. Many groups commented on the changing quality of the space and the atmosphere as we cleaned and painted and especially as we dedicated one room to be a quiet/prayer room. Jack, the hermit from the local parish church, pointed us back to what is most important when he came each week to pray in the quiet room.

Everyone showed us that church is about being human and about trusting in all that we are and may be and the power that is both within us and greater than us. It is about being connected, sharing a space and our dreams and hopes and vulnerability. It is about every person, not about those few who see themselves as faithful keepers of the tradition, who assent to a certain creed, but about those who are open to the gift each person brings. It is big and inclusive, human, not concerned with who is in or out. 'Non-church groups' or 'member' make no sense here. Church is also about change and transformation, the people who are important to us and then must move on, carrying the vision with them and still being part, loved. It is above all about vulnerability and gift, which constantly break us open to new people and ways of being and open to a vibrant and broken world.

I have already mentioned a number of friends who were willing to run with the bread-making idea. There was and still remains a key friendship that has not yet been mentioned but without whom the bread church would not have been possible. Donald Eadie is described on the back of his book *Grain in Winter* as someone who 'has often been in the firing line for advocating justice and respect between people of all faiths, women and men, gay and straight people. In recent years he has lived with a serious spinal condition which forced him to retire early as Chairman of the Birmingham District of the Methodist Church. He has not given up being a much-consulted Methodist minister, leading retreats and writing about spirituality.'

A correspondence via e-mail, entitled rather grandly 'Liverpool Letters', has bounced back and forth between Donald and myself since this project was simply 'a crumb in the eye of God'. Donald's wisdom, and his constant urging to stand back, observe and wait, was initially a great frustration to me when I was geared up for action and change. But of course, Donald is more perceptive than most and has taught me, and so many others, the meaning of the phrase 'wise counsellor'. Throughout the book I include some extracts of the letters to show you what I mean.

From: **Donald**
To: **Barbara**
Date: **17 September 1999**
Subject: **Liverpool Letters**

Thanks for your two letters.

I delight in the bread-making and bread sharing journeys. What a way to begin. And I wonder how this could transform your understanding, experience and celebration of the Eucharist. Perhaps we need to keep asking, 'who are the priests and where are the altars?' and the exploration of Eucharistic living and not just Eucharistic liturgies – the receiving – gratitude and sharing process is a way of living shared by more than the 10.30 gathered few – but more of that another time.

And the notion of a companion as one who breaks the bread with us.

Keep open to what is coming and all the crazy interconnectedness that will and won't make sense at the moment – or perhaps for quite a while – and listen to your feelings of delight, surprise, confusion, anger, bewilderment – and where you come alive.

Peace
Donald

So, in some strange and seemingly disconnected ways a community began to emerge. But how was it possible to know if what was happening was anything at all to do with being church? I can look back now with some notion of what was going on, but truth to tell while it was happening there was very little clarity in the process. Voices, encounters, conversations around the bread table brought both bewilderment and delight, and having the courage to stay open to those possibilities was hard work. So, I encourage you to live this process too and to also have the courage to have more questions than answers in your discovery of what the church might become.

2

The Genius of Bread

Having the courage to become a new community takes a number of different ingredients. In our case there were the physical ingredients that make up bread dough: flour, salt, water, honey, oil, yeast. There were also the emotional ingredients of community and loneliness, of engagement with the city and time for reflection, of questions and muddles. I encourage anyone who wants to embark on such a journey to take time over the quality of all these ingredients. Making Christian communities is not something that can be rushed. We need discernment and patience to select what are the important factors for our particular enterprise. Not everyone will make bread but bread-making for the Somewhere Else community began to be the focus of gathering a group of people who were motivated by the activity and the friendship it brought. This not only encouraged people to have confidence in their own ability but it also brought the nonsense we all live into a safe environment. This community was not so much a place to answer questions as somewhere it was possible to ask them without fear.

We had, of course, only just begun to realize the genius of bread. I guess we will never really get to the bottom of it. I knew some of the biblical resonances that the ingredients held in their memories – leaven in the lump, salt of the earth, oil for anointing and healing, living water. As we began to bake, these ingredients began to take on a life of their own. As soon as we had rooms we began to bake. It was Andrew who persuaded us to extend the kitchen: 'It's the heart of the community so it needs to be the heart of the building.' Initially with a domestic cooker and later with two industrial ovens bought with a grant from the Christian Initiatives Trust, the bread-making developed.

There were some practical questions that led us into new exploration. Where, for instance, do you acquire yeast in the middle of a large city centre? The answer lay not far away in a small yet frantically busy world food shop down the road. Here I discovered little packets of yeast for about 30 pence each. I bought the lot. After a few forays of this kind I was noticed. Dalip approached the curious vicar woman and asked whether perhaps I needed a bigger packet. When I assented he came out with enough freeze-dried yeast for a whole sack of flour. 'Talking of which,' I said, 'you couldn't by any chance get some big sacks of organic Granary flour for us, could you?' Nothing was too much trouble for the family that runs Matta's. Bread flour was supplied as we needed it and was delivered up the street in exchange for a loaf of bread. We soon got to know the family and they became interested in this enterprise that was under way. Sometimes they send sun-dried tomatoes and we make tomato and herb bread for ourselves and for them.

Richard is a retired coroner, a bachelor and lay reader in his church. He has a friend who keeps bees. The friend would provide honey for us in exchange for bread. Richard's friend's honey went into the bread to activate the yeast, and often on the bread at lunchtime to sustain the bakers.

A baker heard of our baking project and came over with a van-load of ingredients, and ran a 'bread bonanza' day for us. He taught us how to make the most of the bubbling yeast and to make sesame seed buns and croissants. In return we helped him through some issues and to a new understanding of an open church community. So it goes on.

Through those early months it was often just Linda and myself who baked. Sometimes others popped in. Sometimes it was just me. Whoever showed up we always made three loaves, kept one and gave the others away, just as we had done in Sheila's kitchen. We set one of the rooms aside for a quiet room. We said our prayers. The builders were in. There was dust everywhere. We waited.

The bookshop News from Nowhere is a women's cooperative that aims to provide literature for minority groups. It has a radically inclusive ethic and has earned a great deal of respect in the local community in the 30 years it has been operating in Liverpool. During its history it has faced compulsory purchase and other opposition but it has survived through the dedication and commitment of its staff and the help of local benefactors. It is to their immense credit that they were prepared to engage with having a Christian community on their premises. Many of the groups that News from Nowhere seeks to advocate have been excluded by the church. As Linda indicated, they have acted not just as landlords to us but also as friends. Our intuition to take on the rooms above the shop soon began to reveal itself as inspired. As the smell of the baking bread drifted down the stairs so people began to drift up the stairs. We got to know Dave at the Windows project on the first floor who worked with children's poetry groups in schools. Jill often came down from the upstairs flat with one-year-old Georgie. We would take down coffee and a hot roll to Paul, who slept on the doorstep with his dog Blue.

Very gradually, the bread-making community grew. There has never been a notice outside the door that declares we are open for bread. People have found their way to us by any number of different routes. News from Nowhere suggested that Storm might find their home with us. Storm is a worship group for gay and lesbian Christians. Tony, the *Big Issue* seller I already knew from the bottom of the street, came with a group of other vendors. Penny brought groups of people with mental health issues. Kerstin just happened to be visiting from Germany. Hilary had been a volunteer at a Christian centre at the Albert Dock that had closed and transferred her volunteering to be with us ... and so it goes on. Five years into the project we are working alongside all kinds of people who come to make bread. There are regularly 20 bakers each Tuesday and Thursday. Yet the original ingredients remain the same – we are called to be here, to make bread, to say our prayers and to wait.

Let me describe to you a typical bread-making morning. A large round table in the middle of the kitchen area is the gathering place for the Somewhere Else community. Some time after 10.30 on a Tuesday and a Thursday people will start to arrive. Let me think of a typical Tuesday. Morris has come with his care assistant Bob, Barbara Greenwood and Stephi have set out the bread ingredients on the table (Barbara is in the process of discerning her vocation, Stephi is a Jesuit volunteer). Carole arrives with her grandson Harry (now two years old). Each person has come with their bread order and Stephi is marking up how many loaves will be made – there is an allowance made to provide lunch for the bakers. Steve arrives. He used to sell the *Big Issue* but is now looking for work. Carole Benn has brought one of her adult students.

We never know who will arrive but the thinking is that 'whoever arrives is whoever God sends'. There is soon a busy-ness as people mix and measure the ingredients into the bowls, as the yeast begins to bubble and foam. Steve goes to buy vegetables for the lunchtime soup.

Just as in Sheila's kitchen, people begin to remember things as they talk easily side by side over their bread bowls. Side-by-side encounters are infinitely less threatening than face-to-face ones. This is a place where it is possible to talk 'out there', rather like companions on a walk are able to converse easily as they go along. Maybe Carl the tutor from the *Big Issue* office has brought someone along for the first time – vendors are credited with a number of sales for the magazine if they come. The vendor has been told by Carl that he is coming to make bread in a church and arrives with justifiable apprehension. Someone is showing him how to mix the ingredients, but soon stands back as Carole encourages him to put his hands right in the mixture and begin to knead the dough. Just as the flour is activated by the honey and yeast so the community becomes activated by laughter and attention. Making bread is great fun and there is soon the bubble of conversation.

It is also good therapy. Tony often gets really angry by the way he is treated on the streets. He has regular customers who are good to him but there are also people who continually give him aggravation. He loves making bread. He says it gives him some respite from all the things that make him angry and he can also give the dough a really good thump.

Someone who lives on his own and is often quite lonely tells us about his ballroom dancing classes. Everyone is chatting. Barbara Greenwood has the kettle on. Steve goes out for a smoke on the doorstep and takes a cup of coffee down for Rob who is there today. We sit down for a chat and drink as the bread in the bowls rises in the proving oven.

By lunchtime the bread has been kneaded again, shaped into tins or arranged on trays as rolls or plaits. Everyone is invited to adjourn to the quiet room for some time of reflection. Some come through, others choose to stay with the bread. There is a time of waiting for the bread to cook. There is a great anticipation as the wonderful aroma fills the room and drifts down the stairs. In the quiet room people sit and begin to feel calmer; they are invited not to speak but to let the sounds and aroma around them be their focus. It is never silent in the city centre, we can usually hear someone on their mobile phone or a car radio outside. We can hear Rob calling to sell the *Big Issue* and the gulls on the roof opposite. After a while a Bible passage may be read. People are invited to comment if they wish but not to interrupt each other. Thoughts are offered and listened to without comment. Prayers are then offered into the silence. Some people may choose to light candles, some may prefer to remain still or silent. Little Harry lights a candle and says a prayer for 'Mummy and Daddy and the baby in the tummy.' Steve, an avid reader of the newspaper, usually has a current situation on his mind.

Heather has now joined us on her lunch hour from Lewis's and Big Harry has arrived on his bike having cycled up from the Albert Dock where he works on a sailing ship. Some people want to light a candle but it is too difficult for them to venture into the middle of a room full of people. Others have trouble not thinking out loud. Whoever leads the group needs to let these issues rest in the silence and to be sensitive to body language and the respect for each other's space.

Because the bread-making process has natural pauses in it there is a rhythm to the day which gives time and attention to the community of individuals who gather. One of the things people seem to appreciate most about the whole process is that it incorporates space – space to think, space to be listened to, space just to be. It often strikes me that what we offer is the simplest thing in the world. We give people time and attention – it is just that on the whole we live in a society that isn't very good at it.

Returning to the bread table, the loaves are ready to come out from the oven. Everyone wants to identify their own and see how it turned out. Soup is ready along with fruit salad, cheese and the lunchtime rolls – brown, white and Granary. We are all hungry and dive in greedily. One day, one of the *Big Issue* guys stood up and objected. 'I thought this was a church, aren't we going to say a prayer?' Rather taken aback I said to him, 'Sure, do you have a prayer you want to say?' Undaunted he shut his eyes and led us in an 'Our Father' and a 'Hail Mary', then he said, 'Thank you, God, for this place and this bread and this Barbara that I love. Amen.'

Mysteriously, although everybody's loaf is different, the bread is invariably good. Everyone is very pleased with themselves. The sense of achievement is tangible.

So, bread is made and given away. We don't sell our loaves. Considering bread to be a gift to us from God, it is our gift to share. It is extraordinary where our bread gets to! I once met someone in London who had received a loaf. Usually, though, it travels in and around Liverpool. Tony delivers loaves to some of the shop assistants on Bold Street who buy his magazines. Barbara Greenwood has a regular order with some of her pastoral group on Wirral. Penny and I took a whole bagful to a meeting of the Health Action Zone. Faced with a group of health workers from around the region, Penny introduced herself: 'My name is Penny, I am transgendered and that means I am different. I make bread at Bold Street and it's great to be there. It's one of the few places I can be accepted for who I am and it's great fun.' I think the bread we gave out that day had more impact than a whole lot of PowerPoint presentations.

Process

One of the many things the bread is teaching us is to understand process. Bread won't be hurried, and nor can people. The twice-weekly gathering of people to make bread has a rhythm to it which is not limited by a timescale. On warm days the bread rises faster; when there are more bakers a longer time is needed for mixing and shaping. Some days not many turn up and we wonder where everyone has gone. We have had to learn to work with whoever it is God sends. Sometimes we have very few people and we catch ourselves apologizing. It was Col who put us right on this: 'What's the point of apologizing because some people didn't turn up – I'm here so you can work with me!'

There are times when the groups who arrive are full of confidence; on other occasions they are afraid or diffident. Usually there is a mixture of the shy and the bumptious. It is impossible to overestimate the skill required in facilitating such groups. Quietly and firmly, those who welcome others around the bread table must read when to encourage and when to leave alone, to give people space without leaving anyone out. We don't always get it right. One member of our community, for instance, has difficulty in reading social cues so he tends to interrupt or draws loud attention to himself. Someone else has a challenge with anger management. These two often antagonize each other and sometimes get near to blows. By gentle intervention and the ability to withdraw to a quieter space if necessary, these challenges are usually negotiated with a great degree of good humour and firmness. But sometimes we just can't sort it. We have to acknowledge that we are a challenging collection of people around the bread table and we sometimes cannot make it right.

Some of the most difficult moments come when racist or sexist remarks are made. Maybe these are made by someone who ought to know better, but sometimes the person who has spoken is not able to read social cues sufficiently well to understand when comments are not appropriate. Learning to challenge in ways that are also inclusive is very difficult territory, as it can appear that the person who challenges is assuming the moral high ground. We have struggled particularly with people with mental health issues. It is so hard to know how much of their antisocial behaviour is attributable to their illness. We try not to talk about people in their absence but we have had to have a few summit meetings to discuss how to challenge behaviour without excluding individuals. As Marie asked with a twinkle in her eye, 'Why is it that excluded people are so difficult to include?'

Sometimes, if I am helping to facilitate a group, I encourage people by saying, 'I'll believe in you and you believe in the bread.' Often people get quite possessive about 'their' bowl of dough and it is necessary to respect each person as they make bread in their own individual way. The only really difficult people to deal with are 'experts'!

Strangers meet side by side as they work at their bread dough. They soon fall into conversation. As the months have gone by we have worked with any number of different groups of people – some come as a self-defined group, while others come as individuals and join a group of strangers. Maybe one of the most curious groups was one in which the participants knew each other well but only through conversation over the Internet. They were both intimate acquaintances and strangers.

In the months I wandered around the city centre, I began to appreciate that it was an honour when someone gave you their name. To know someone's name is a powerful thing and so we must be careful not to demand names. When we offer our own name to strangers we need to understand that they might choose to remain nameless. Our continuing challenge is to respect each person's autonomy so that they are free to enter and leave the group on their own terms. No one needs to stay until the end, no one is obliged to answer a direct question. All we are doing is offering space and making bread.

One of the hardest things about this process is that people do leave. For me, that was particularly difficult at the beginning, when we were only a tiny community. Both Sheila and Linda moved away for family and work commitments in other parts of the country. And there was something deep inside me that still wanted to measure 'success' by counting heads. I had to learn to forget about the numbers game to continually remind myself that we are only here for now. We are not building something for all eternity but simply endeavouring to be present to the bread-making and the people God sends today. This concept was helped by our early conversations in which the Somewhere Else community made a resolution to go for quality and not quantity, for depth rather than width. It is both a challenge and a freedom to work in this way. We try to be present to people without worrying about numbers. We have found that one side-effect of this is that more people come!

It is a challenge when it comes to the expectations of the wider church. As some congregations face the future without a minister, this small group of bread-makers demands a great deal of individual attention. There is a financial cost that does not see easy returns. Believing in people is hugely demanding. It also lays us open to being used or being considered a 'soft touch'. Some people will lie to us or continually ask for money. Promises are broken. Being let down is a frequent phenomenon. We are always struggling to let go of our disappointments without recriminations. We do not always achieve an easy path to forgiveness.

There are both advantages and disadvantages to working with what some might describe as a 'temporary emotional community'. The concept of a 'temporary emotional community' runs counter to the way many churches engage with a process of encouraging discipleship. We are working with a different paradigm or 'story image'. The image we engage with is less of a 'sheepfold' – where all may be 'safely gathered in' – but a 'watering hole' that people may visit and leave refreshed. If it is the case that we are a place where people can enter and leave as they need then there is a built-in instability in the community. This can challenge our sense of safety. Our church instinct tends to want to gather people in and keep them. Postmodern society tends to configure gathering in a different way. People are wary of being trapped. They need to see their exits. If people are free to leave it seems they are more inclined to stay.

This is most important with people who have struggled with issues of inclusion. The church has often been implicated in some way. Many survivors of abuse, for instance, will cite the church explicitly as the source of the abuse or implicitly as deaf to disclosure. People with mental health issues are often alienated by church communities when their behaviour fails to conform to the 'norm', and the story of the exclusion of the gay community is too well documented for me to add more clarity to the picture. In short, for very good reasons, church can be a frightening place. To enter into conversation with Christians is a situation in which the power should remain firmly in the hands of the fearful.

The transformative nature of this encounter is always surprising. On many occasions people have written to me saying: 'Thanks for the day bread-making. It has really changed the way I look at things. I feel life will never be the same again.' This strikes me as extraordinary because we have done something that seems so simple. Yet there is a basic human delight in engaging with such a creative thing from within a context of acceptance and safety. More often than not this delight isn't simply about a cookery experience. It strikes very deeply into the human spirit. People are empowered by it. They feel better about themselves, through laughter and creativity. More than this, they go on to begin to question what is important to them and how they might make life-giving choices.

This is an intriguing phenomenon. Why would something as simple as a loaf of bread move people to ask questions about God? I suspect that part of the answer is in the intention of the Somewhere Else community. We are simply called to be present and to make bread because we believe that is what God has called us into. We are not there to promote a set of doctrines or to persuade people into our beliefs. We don't have a hidden agenda. We can say simply, 'This is who we are'. Because this is so simple and transparent, we begin to earn people's trust. This is a safe enough environment to not be sure about things. There is room to ask questions. People will do their utmost to listen and to appreciate the other's points of view. I think this is why people get so excited about bread.

Because we are not particularly anxious about numbers we find that some people are drawn in to greater depth. Some members are not able to come during working hours to make bread on Tuesdays and Thursdays. Others valued the bread-making times but wanted another space where it was possible to talk openly around some of the issues raised around the bread table. As a result, one member began a faith-sharing group on a Tuesday night. In this group the manner of engagement is slightly more explicit. They have drawn up a code of respect which, in short, says, 'You can say what you like without being interrupted or criticized provided that's how you are with everyone else.' The group has grown in numbers and in the range of topics addressed – recent topics have included 'Being trapped' and a 'Reflection on the route of the number 89 bus'! There has also been a request for more worship so that there are now gatherings for worship most Sundays. We have also celebrated two gay blessings, two weddings and recently Ben and Penny have both been baptized.

A mixed up gift

From:	**Barbara**
To:	**Donald**
Date:	**19 January 2001**
Subject:	**Liverpool Letters**

Liverpool is quiet after the Christmas scrum (although I notice Creme Eggs in the shops already). Yesterday we celebrated the beginning of the Week of Prayer for Christian Unity by holding the Covenant service at our place. A small but good gathering – celebrated with the noise of the city outside and from inside the smell of baking bread.

Various callers rang the bell yesterday and every time I opened the door the person standing there wasn't one I expected! One classic moment was when it should have been a structural engineer and turned out to be a guy trying to book a room for Alcoholics Anonymous ... it was a while before I figured out who I was talking to!

Bread-making mixes all sorts of things together. It mixes people with very different life experiences. It challenges our stereotypes. It also reminds us of issues of justice, among ourselves and across the world. It mixes the boundaries between seriousness and light-heartedness. Through the bread we begin to see that the complexity of the world is a source of delight and challenge. Having the courage to live in this mixed up way is harder than engaging with groups that are clearly defined. The mixing is an important feature of an emerging community. Diversity is a gift.

One of the many ways bread-making mixes things up is in the synthesis of creative and physical activity. This is not unusual in a creative context. Sculptors and artists know that to make a piece of work out of stone or to paint a large canvas is about transferring the concept from initial design through the medium of physical exertion. We are, however, less inclined to do this in churches. Unless you are involved with liturgical dance or drama, Sunday mornings tend to be fairly sedentary experiences. By contrast, bread-making is physically active. It uses the whole of the body to pummel the dough and to move it between table and oven. People are often surprised how shattered they are after a morning with the bread team.

Engaging the whole of our bodies in a creative process begins to integrate the connections between the outside self that we present to the world and our innermost feelings. Rather in the way that walking up a hill side by side with a companion will enable a conversation to unfold because the physical body is active, so engagement with bread-making helps a conversation to be released. I think the trigger for this process is memory.

Bread stimulates all the senses. The touch of the dough is reminiscent of many things – and as it moves from a sticky mess to a round, smooth lump it has a tangible sense of transformation. Most evocative of all is the aroma of bread. From its yeasty origins to the warm wholesome aroma of the cooked loaf, it is adept at triggering our memories. Of course, not all these memories are necessarily positive. Strong childhood memories for good and bad can be evoked. As memory bridges the gap between what our hands are doing and what our heads are thinking, stories emerge.

Bread responds well to heavy-handedness. I once made the mistake of encouraging a young person who was reluctantly prodding the dough with one finger to 'imagine it's your least favourite teacher'. I had to call a truce, but it was good bread!

Another mixture that bread reminds me of confusion of categories of church. We are prone to think of congregations as being evangelical, radical or liberal. We have developed stereotypes for each of these 'categories' that enable us to slot people into a convenient box. We may have views about gay people that will have developed from a number of influences. We probably have a political stance that informs the way we view the world. Around the bread table people who would describe themselves in many different ways meet in a different space. It is a place of human encounter in which we attempt to hold these differences without judgement.

When we first opened our kitchens we had a 'bread-warming party'. I wasn't quite sure how many I had invited, so we set the room out so that it was possible to make bread as you walked around the table. People arrived, took off their coats, washed their hands and were given a bowl of flour. As their bread progressed so did they, so there was space for the newest arrival by the door. In the end 60 people made bread that night! There was a complete mix. People from Storm, some *Big Issue* guys, the president of the Liverpool Association of Chartered Accountants, a pension fund manager, a member of 'Moral Rearmament', some children, an Anglican priest, a policeman ... It was a random jumble of humanity. Probably the only person who knew everyone else was me and as I glanced around the room I could see miracle upon miracle as the most unlikely people were talking to each other as friends. The word 'companion' means 'together in bread'.

Making bread and giving it away is a gentle, personable activity. It is also subversive. In a capitalist economy that relies on trade, giving something as essential as bread as a gift is counter-cultural. When there is a panic about supply and demand, people go out and buy bread. Even in a petrol crisis bread sales go up. There is something about having bread that makes us conscious of our own tentative survival. If we were starving and had bread then at least our children would be fed. It is a very deep human instinct.

We are all aware that two-thirds of the world's population is undernourished. Our hoarding of bread is a symbol of our inability to share resources. In many parts of the world women in particular struggle to make scant provision for their families. While at the Somewhere Else community most of us are not reliant on the bread for our personal survival (although some are) there is a sense of solidarity with people for whom this is the case. In this way this little community stands as a radical counter-sign, set as it is in the heart of the retail and business community of one of Britain's larger cities.

'Bethlehem' means 'house of bread'. Not the gingerbread house out of some fairy tale, but the place where the invisible God showed his face. Even modern Bethlehem is a town continually faced with issues of war and injustice. It is a place of struggle. We find that bread-making also brings us to our own struggles. It is not just a friendly time of recreation which amuses us with some distracting activity, it is about the reality of human struggle, in our faces and across different economic and cultural experiences. Here is another consequence of mixing things up in this way. In a non-threatening, yet profoundly challenging sense, bread-making is political.

On one occasion Storm had come to make bread. We were all being extremely politically correct. The group members were mostly gay men but there were one or two women. We were talking about everything except sexuality. Everyone was checking out everyone else. It was when two loaves fused together in the oven that the whole evening took off! We laughed so much our sides ached, we couldn't speak. Someone made a comment and we were off again. Our eyes were streaming tears. Once we had got over the release of tension and the bread was set to cool on the side in the kitchen a new, relaxed conversation began. We talked of the exclusion of the gay community from many churches. Stories were told of hurts and struggles. One lad who had some difficulty with words began, 'My name is Don and I have trouble speaking clearly, if you have trouble understanding me ... well, tough!' There followed a story of such sensitivity and resilience despite such misunderstanding and prejudice that we all listened deeply and intensely. Through moments such as these we discover that the community is growing to be both light-hearted and deep-spirited.

My White Dress
A poem by Marie

What about my white dress, my marquee,
    my four-tier cake?
What about the parties, the presents, the
    endless congratulations?
What about my honeymoon, my ring, the
    horse and carriage?
Where's my Mum dabbing her tears
My Dad bursting with pride as we sail
    down the aisle?
What about my white dress, my rite of
    passage, my prophecy of gender?

If I'm not going to the church then where
    am I going?
If I don't know where I'm going how will
    I know I've arrived?
Who will welcome me and celebrate my
    arrival?
What is it I am journeying towards if it's
    not my white dress?

It's not a white dress, it's a blank page
Free of the restraining corsetry and
    submissive veil.

I will arrive because I have already
　started my journey.
I will paint the landscape on my way.
Eruptions of ecstasy and sadness will be
　my milestones.
No affirmation and congratulation to seal
　us, you're already at my side.
Carte blanche, freedom from a life of
　expectation.

It was never my white dress.

It seems to me that a community such as this hits a place that is often too deep for words. Stories such as Don's and Marie's come from deep wells and bubble up with tears and laughter. It is another aspect of our mixed up community.

In the early days of Somewhere Else we were often accused of 'not being real church'. It was Col who gave us the answer to this accusation: 'It's more real than any church you know!' It's true. We hit reality in a very deep sense. If your mother had been a 16-year-old prostitute and you were adopted without really knowing her, or if your father abused you so remorselessly that 30 years later you were only just beginning to tell the story, then this is real stuff. Yet curiously, from out of such reality comes a deep resilience of the human spirit that gives zest and joy to life. It is not to deny that these things happened but that somehow, despite everything, today is a gift. Life is here and now, confusing, messed up, contradictory, yet it is life.

The most wonderful thing about mixing and kneading in the bread-making community is that it is so simple. Making bread is ridiculously easy, and accessible to anyone. James is blind; he likes to smell the mixture and is amazed at its texture and warmth.

Little Harry moulds his dough into shapes and takes them home for Mummy and Daddy. Morris works with Bob to make superb bread, although he likes a bit of a sit down half-way through. Morris's whole community enjoys his loaves and he is able to take one for his mum.

It challenges us more profoundly than many of us have been challenged before. Is there a limit on our generosity? How do we include people who really annoy us? How do we challenge racist remarks? How do we acknowledge the reality of abuse without demeaning or compromising those who have not only survived but also learned to flourish? These are some of the questions that are emerging for us.

Then we eat it! Our bread is particularly good with soup or cheese or hot with butter and jam. We enjoy it. We relish it. We put on weight. The bread doesn't last long, not just because it is fresh and yummy but also because it contains no preservatives. All flour, even organic flour, has some additives required by law but manufactured bread has other ingredients added to give it a 'shelf life'. We only use natural ingredients. We know what is in our bread and we are pleased that it is the best. This is not just about a middle-class desire to add purity to our diets. There is a real need to provide the best of all possible options particularly for those members of our community with chaotic eating patterns. It is important to sit and eat around a table, to converse as we eat and to sense that we are worth nourishing. There is wholesomeness in the experience of sharing bread together around a communal table. We are proud of what we have made and it is a good pride.

We believe that this pride in our bread builds our confidence as individuals and as a community. Marie says, 'It is the first time I've really been proud of my church. I want to tell everyone about it. It's a cool place and I want everyone to share what I have.' Sitting and sharing, learning to trust each other, learning to be attentive to each other's needs is calming and deeply satisfying. Tony's soup is the highlight of the week – he always makes gallons of it! He comes in from his *Big Issue* pitch and chops vegetables with such pleasure and satisfaction. He says it helps him to feel calm and to chill out.

In this way bread nourishes both our bodies and our spirits. We know that it is holy food – not only because it is wholesome but also because it helps us to value the whole of ourselves. Our bodies matter, they are not to be denied. They deserve good food that is simple and nutritious. Our spirits thrive when we are seen as whole people with all our struggle and wonder. If we can sense we are worth attending to then in turn we are able to attend to other people. So we grow to look for meaning in our lives and to ask questions about why things are as they are. We begin to open up spaces of silence and prayer in our souls. Some integrity unfurls in our lives.

Echoes

There are so many references in the Scriptures to bread and to its significance to human existence. There are so many echoes of the Gospels in our little community. I suppose the story that has most significance to myself and to the Somewhere Else community is the encounter of the disciples with the risen Jesus on the road to Emmaus. There are several reasons why this is so. It is significant that the story unfolds as the two travellers take leave of the city – just as the faithful congregation of the Methodist Central Hall in Liverpool did so many years later. Now, as then, all must have seemed lost. 'We had hoped he was the Lord', they say rather bleakly. Hopes dashed, vision evaporated, tired and despondent, they are giving up and going home and it is at this moment that Jesus falls into step beside them.

I often sense that we anticipate Jesus arriving with a great fanfare. There will be a conversion experience, a sudden revelation of certainty, a moment of faith. More often than not we overlook those who walk in step beside us and who, simply by their presence and patience, wait for us to recognize what is happening. In the story, Jesus comes as a stranger. They are friendly enough towards him but they don't really see him until he does something that is familiar – that is, when he breaks bread. Like the travellers on the road we can hear Scriptures explained until the cows come home but unless we make the connection between what we hear and what we experience then we will not see who travels alongside us. Jesus waits and walks, keeps faith with the travellers until they are moved to offer hospitality to him at the end of their journey.

At the meal, when all the words of the day have been spent, they are finally able to look Jesus in the eye and understand who has been with them all this time. Then their lives are transformed, they are energized and excited, they want to tell others, they want to return to the city. I see in this story of 2,000 years ago that Jesus knew intuitively the genius of bread.

Ben is learning the Lord's Prayer. He has it on a piece of paper and reads it during prayer time. Ben was baptized a few months ago – he is a gay man from a Muslim country and an asylum seeker. He was brought up as a Muslim but has found Christian faith through the bread church. He came to this country in the back of a lorry. He has a job giving out leaflets which earns him some money and a few unwanted encounters with dogs. Ben says that it is in the hands of Providence if he is allowed to stay here – he says, 'What will be, will be.'

When we say the Lord's Prayer together we connect with Christians since the days of Jesus. Not all in our community know the words; some knew them once as children, and to others like Ben they are unfamiliar. When we say, 'Give us this day our daily bread', we all know what we are talking about. It is about having sufficient bread to enjoy and nourish our day, about being able to be part of a community that looks for a way of being Christian that is neither greedy nor stingy. It is about appreciating the gift of God's bread, for our bodies and our souls each day and for each other.

That is not to say we always get it right – we most certainly do not. We are not some ideal of a church community. We can be jealous and mean-spirited. We can panic or fail to see the bigger picture. That is why I have come to understand 'Forgive us our trespasses as we forgive those who trespass against us' in a different way. Rather than understanding my forgiveness to be somehow linked with the way I forgive others, I see that God forgives me *at the same time* as I try to forgive others and myself. As I engage with the struggle of finding out what forgiveness means, both personally and as part of a community, so God engages with us to bring us to a broader and deeper understanding of his grace.

And the kingdom we pray for? Well, certainly it is a future hope, but occasionally we glimpse it right in front of our eyes around the bread table.

The day 25 people were coming to have a meeting and expecting lunch and I forgot to mention it was a day when we knew about feeding the 5,000. Apparently (I had gone out) the group adjourned from another room and plonked themselves down at the table where the ten or so bread-makers were taken by surprise. Of course there was enough to go round – not by some miraculous multiplication of loaves but rather by an inherent desire on the part of the community to share what it had (and to water down soup!)

Something has always struck me as odd about that bread and fish story – one of the few stories to appear in all four Gospels. Who was it that went to the picnic that day with empty baskets? The story tells of Jesus giving responsibility to the disciples to solve their own problem: 'All these people are here and there is no food.' When they took responsibility and came up with five loaves and two fishes, then Jesus breaks the bread and all are fed – and there were baskets full left over. So someone went to the picnic expecting there to be more than enough. When our surplus guests turned up there was an expectation that there would be enough because we were prepared to take responsibility for the shortfall. God has never left us short – more than that, there has always been much more than we expected. We are learning to be followers who come with nothing and expect great things.

Living Eucharist

As Donald predicted, I am beginning to understand 'Eucharist' more as a verb than a noun. I want to talk of 'eucharistic living'. That is a living out of our experience that transforms our way of relating with each other. A way of giving thanks for the otherness of the other as a gift. To live eucharistically is to acknowledge that there is the possibility of an authentic inclusive way to live our lives. It is a rejection of any ideals that by definition exclude some and label others as failures. Issues are given faces. It is an encouragement to the church to live with incompleteness as a gift in such a way that brokenness is seen as an accepted way to flourish. As Donald says:

> Eucharistic living is about learning to be open, open to receiving the gifts of God through both dark and light, through both the creative and the destructive, through the essential 'otherness' of those who are different. Eucharistic living is about an openness to receiving that could include the possibility of bewildering transformation, about gratitude and about sharing. (Eadie, 1999, p. 13)

Eucharist is easy enough to see in the baking, breaking and sharing of bread as a fragmented community meets and disperses. Now I see that there is also the wine of laughing and dancing. As we recognize the nuanced and struggling gift of the other we are also given the possibility of a deep, almost reckless, delight. Such delight comes from claiming, not denying, the struggle. We claim not only our struggle but also our celebration of being in the company of others. It is about being embodied people, remembered and loved by God even in our oddness and incompleteness. So, the ordinary bread and wine of a strange community gains the possibility of transformation not just for us but to the ends of the earth. The mystery is in this extraordinary ordinary mystery among extraordinary ordinary people.

7 February 2001

A young woman came up from the bookshop today – to hire a room for a women's group – she said, 'I feel so much better since I've been eating your bread – do you put prayers in it or something?'

I think it is right to be suspicious of new communities. We can readily be sucked into cults by unscrupulous leaders or sign up to groups that might entrap and do us harm. We can lead vulnerable people into difficulties if power goes to our heads. It is always important that we are checking out our authenticity and accountability. What are some of the hallmarks we should look for in discerning a genuine place of the Spirit? How do we know that Somewhere Else is in fact a church?

Is this a praying community that holds fast to the Scriptures and celebrates the sacraments? To this I can assuredly say 'yes'. The Bible informs the very heart of our community. Although some of the decisions we make may be seen by more conservative Christians to be controversial, we are assured that we are informed by scholarship in our discernment of biblical truths. In fact, the gospel makes more sense to me now than it ever has before. We struggle with the Scriptures, we read them and let them stand alongside our experience.

Is this a sacramental community? We celebrate the sacrament of Holy Communion more often and with a much deeper understanding than many Sunday morning congregations. Bread-sharing is not a ritualized activity or separated from our daily experience. It is the heart of who we are. As we appreciate the genius of bread more, its ordinariness and its holiness, so our celebration of Eucharist becomes deeper and richer. I understand 'real presence' to be the wonder of God that I have seen at work in this community yet is always mysteriously aloof.

Is this a community that looks to traditional wisdom for its accountability? The leadership of the church – initially me but now a leadership team – is both mutually accountable and accountable to the

Methodist tradition of which we are a part. We don't always obey all the rules of the denomination but we are aware when we move into difficult territory. We take responsibility for these decisions. We are particularly scrupulous about our safeguarding policy – we will do everything in our power to make sure that all people on our premises are safe from harm.

Is this a community in which we can see the fruits of the Spirit? Yes, indeed, we see people flourishing, working on their faith, demonstrating gifts of the spirit and sharing God's grace. One result of this is a bubbling-up of vocations – to ordained ministry but also to store chaplaincies and secular roles. Maybe surprisingly, we have had two people come to us for baptism and two couples for marriage. Three members of the community are embarking on Foundation Training for ministry this year. There are other visible signs of transformation – growth in confidence, in the ability to manage anger, to make life choices. In all these ways we sense that we are a gospel community, walking with the Spirit but always with our eyes open.

So the courage to be a new Christian community comes in small and gentle ways. What we have discovered is that mixing people together around a common activity is a way in which close, unforced friendships can flourish. Being a safe space where people are free to air their doubts and troubles is important, and crucial to this is permission to leave. We have found that, rather than this being 'a new approach to church', as if in some way we were creating something out of nothing, actually God has approached us and opened the Scriptures through our connection with strangers. We are learning not to fear the chaos of a group of people meeting for the first time. We are encouraged that all this is not dependent on our own ability but that community opens up gently if we are faithful to our core vision. So I encourage you to look at ways to cross conventional boundaries. This is not a reckless dive into uncharted water but rather a reaching out to each other in friendship. When we look lovingly into each other's eyes then we see how God is indeed ahead of us.

A poem by Avis

From honey and oil, flour salt, water and
    yeast
Coming together, the dough
Was formed.
Then shaped by the actions of my hands.
A rhythmic kneading, turning sides and
    centre
Inside to out
And outside to in,
A malleable medium
Receiving the undulations of my palm
A Henry Moore sculpture in a mixing
    bowl
But warm,
Warm to and from my touch
Absorbing not only energy
But thoughts and feelings
The history of my working week
Which, hidden yet holy,
Later will be shared

3

The Silence that Calls to Us

From: **Donald**
To: **Barbara**
Date: **18 August 2001** (in response to a journal written over the summer months)
Subject: **Liverpool Letters**

Tell me more about the 'space somewhere else' group to include people of faith that can't find a place in the church. Crucial and wonderful and thank God you are into it. What form, what issues, where do they emerge from and who, what of the search for a common human language, of images, rituals?

Gay blessings? There can be music to face but also music of another kind!

And the call to a particular place ... I also wonder about this ... and I wonder about what it means for those who live with the implications of our sense of call ... our children, cats dogs and all and our mothers and fathers and brothers and sisters – and what of their sense of call?

And the call to become who we are – where we are – the call to become our name.

And the need for place and a people to confirm our identity – and what those contexts awaken within us and draw into being within us ... and can it be possible that anywhere else will be a place of flourishing – a different flourishing from part of us waiting to be awakened?

A liturgy of everything

While I want to encourage you to explore new ways to be people in communities of faith I also want to encourage wisdom. Just because people are together and find satisfaction in what they are doing does not mean that what emerges is necessarily wholesome. We may struggle with the concept of church in its inherited form as it has become overlaid with so many of the trappings of institutions but there are important hallmarks to genuine Christian communities that should not be lost.

One of these distinctive hallmarks is an engagement with liturgy. Liturgy is the shape we give our worship. Denied the usual forum in which worship is exercised, my first year in the city centre lost its sense of shape. I had no easy rhythm to the week or to the seasons. Easter and Christmas were much alike. In truth that is how it is for most of the population for most of the time. There may be a kind of secular rhythm to life, shopping on Saturday, lie-in on Sunday, meal out once a month ... but where is God in all this? If, as I had speculated when I first embarked on this enterprise, God is as much 'at large' in the day-to-day affairs of the world as within the institutions of faith, where is the liturgy of the city?

In Chapter 1 I noted that there were places where there was praise of creation, where people could tell their story to a counsellor, where the physical body and mental state could find healing. All these things have echoes of liturgy about them. So why did the people who came to Somewhere Else ask for more worship? In fact, they continue to ask for more worship, as if they cannot get enough of it. Curious, in days when most church attendances are plummeting.

I don't have a direct answer to this, but I think there is a clue in the parallel request for space.

Margaret put it something like this: 'I went to church on Sunday. I'd had a hell of a week. The priest talked from one end of the service to the other. It's not that what he said wasn't valid, it was just that I had no room in my head for anything else. I needed to put something down first before I could think about what he was saying.' It seems that the resonance our community has with the art gallery and the counselling room is that it is a place that gives people space. That is, both physical and emotional space. As we sense we have more space, room to manoeuvre, then we can move into more and deeper silence. It is as though God breaks through the cracks in our lives to meet us between our thoughts.

This space is not necessarily about inactivity. Liturgical engagement is an active process. We need to be in a place where we can make choices. This involves taking responsibility for our own needs. It sounds like a very adult thing to do, but in fact it is probably Morris who has learning difficulties and little Harry who is just two years old who most often show us the way.

I met Morris at a memorial service at the residential home where he lives. A number of his community make bread. When someone died unexpectedly they asked if I would go to take a service of remembrance. Apparently I had won their 'golden vicar award'! Anyway, we had a very special time of remembering their friend with photographs, tears and laughter and then I suggested that we might light some little candles. When the candles were lit, Morris suddenly said, 'I want to go to church, I like church!' This was the source of some surprise as no one knew Morris had ever been to church and it was quite out of character for him to declare that he wanted to go anywhere. Morris makes bread regularly now and loves to come through to the quiet room to light a candle. He never holds back on what he wants to say, in fact he usually shows his care assistant what to do. Sometimes Morris wants to stay in the quiet room when everyone else has moved away.

Little Harry has a whale of a time building with bricks, helping his granny with the dough and greeting everyone as they arrive. He knows all the bread-makers by name and notices if anyone is missing. He is by far the best church door steward I've ever had! Sometimes he has a sleep on a big cushion in a corner while the bread-making happens around him. When it comes to prayer time little Harry is right in there.

Morris and Harry show us something essential about liturgy. They show us how to connect our physical and soul needs within a pattern of being. They express their needs very directly and show us how the balance of activity and prayer can become a seamless garment.

This is a curious facet of a Methodist community because it reflects a rule of life that comes from a monastic tradition. The Benedictines knew how to balance their prayers, their activity and their study throughout the day. This balancing of all the facets of our being is, I am coming to believe, the source of a living liturgy. In this way liturgy is not an alien pattern of prayer to impose upon our daily lives at the expense of the things we would rather do. On the contrary, prayer and activity can be the medium in which our lives our lived. This balancing is mindful of the things that are happening around us, to our feelings, to our material surroundings. I think we only get to this understanding if we are really attentive to the depth of our own silence. Liturgy is not something that we do but rather something that comes to us in the pattern of our days.

The monks also give us a clue about the reading of the Scriptures. The word is read into the silence as the monastic community is eating. There is no opportunity for comment or interpretation, the word just rests in the space. As they live their days in prayer, study and physical labour, so this word rests with them. The word of God has its own life and stands in solidarity with our lives in a place that is beyond words. Again, a curious discovery for someone who stands in a tradition where preaching is at the heart of worship. There is nothing like a Methodist gathering for filling a space with words! I am not saying that preaching is wrong, nor am I saying that at Somewhere Else we are usually silent – we most certainly are not – but we are being asked, as church, by people who look for meaning in their lives, to let the silence rest with the word. It is in this creative yet silent dialogue that the gospel comes to life. This is a great moment of trust for us. How do we know that people will get an authentic view of the Scriptures? How will they learn about the traditions of the church that have stood the test of time?

One day we were exploring the passage when Jesus goes into the temple and declares the day of jubilee – where the prisoners are set free and the blind given their sight. Tony took the part of Jesus. He was very bossy. He told the prisoner to get up and stop hanging around in prison. He told the blind man he could see and what was he waiting for. After the time together we told Tony that we had difficulty with Jesus being so assertive, we didn't really think of him like that. 'Ah,' says Tony, 'your Jesus isn't the same as my Jesus.' Indeed, it is in the spaces that we learn.

In order to have sufficient room to move around on Sunday mornings we use all the rooms for worship. The quiet room is designated as silent space, the middle room has the Sunday papers and a selection of books, the large kitchen is a place to chatter and make lunch. Starting in the quiet room some poem or reading is shared and people are invited to use a designated time in whatever way they choose. Some will opt to spend an hour in silence, others will move from one space to another – a chance to read and pray the Sunday papers, for instance. In the kitchen there is always a lively dialogue and also art materials, should anyone choose to write or draw. I usually opt for silence. It suits my introverted personality type and also safeguards me from interaction with people's difficulties. I need to worship too. In a rather superior way I was initially quite irritated with people who just chattered away in the big room. Yet when we all reconvened to share any thoughts or reflections on the morning, everyone contributed in equal measure.

This has shown me the need to engage with worship in the way that God leads us rather than in a prescriptive format. Lonely people often need to talk, active people need to rest. Some need to be able to talk to know what they are thinking; others need deep reflective spaces to process what they have already thought. For some it is useful to put things on a piece of paper, others need the input of the written word. All this is possible with room to move.

It is curious for a community of the silenced to look for silence. For many of us, myself included, it has been a long and lonely journey to find our voices. We need to be 'listened into speech' like many of the marginal groups that struggle with an authoritarian and patriarchal church. But it is because we know that we are going to be listened to that we feel safe to embark upon silence. When we have the choice about our own silence then we can set out on the journey into our own souls.

It can be in the place of silence that the God who is so often silent is ultimately most present. The best of friends are able to sit in an understanding silence that can last for ages. A place of understanding where there is nothing to prove gets us off our bandwagons. There is a place for serious engagement here. In silence there is room for us to meet each other within our own amazing humanity. This is always something beyond words. We are crafted and shaped in complexity and nuance. There is a wonder and ambiguity to being human that is deeper than we can or should articulate. In silence the curious 'I am' of each of us is free to meet the ultimate 'I am' of eternity.

Challenges

Maybe it is a peculiarity of a city centre that such a wide variety of people find their way to the door. I certainly could not have predicted the differences in the people who visit us or settle with us for a while. It is a gift. Like most gifts you have to be prepared to receive it.

Col and I now laugh about the first day she came. She was working with vulnerable young adults and was looking for a room for work with young street workers. Church could not have been further from her mind. I on the other hand had an appointment with a Turkish asylum seeker. Between the door and my office we both had to do a quick rethink.

Not only is this variety of people a continuing surprise and gift, it is also challenging. One day we had a film crew wanting to make a documentary about Liverpool's 'Year of Faith'. I was sitting on a chair with a rather bright light shining in my face with a presenter asking me such questions as, 'What is different about the Methodist faith?' (where to begin!) while behind me I could hear that little Harry was feeling unusually unsettled, and there was all sorts of chatter and laughter. The doorbell rang and it was a Somalian charity worker wondering whether or not we could support his village which was struggling to find enough food to survive. That kind of mix is not unusual.

Maybe the biggest challenges are people with mental health issues. Someone in a manic phase of manic depression is almost impossible to hold within such a fragile community. Similarly, a person with strong homophobic or racist views will soon be challenged and may decide to leave. On any day, I suppose we can only do our best. Chaos has a curious way of working itself into something creative and sometimes it is at the moment when we feel we are not in control that there is a surprising connection. But sometimes it's just awful.

I am in a place now where I don't think being gay is anything out of the ordinary. If gay people were not welcome at Somewhere Else our whole community would be hugely impoverished. Gender issues do, however, influence the way a group works, especially if there are overt heterosexual assumptions. Sexuality should be a cause for rejoicing and delight so we won't allow people to get away with sexist remarks. We will challenge anything that hints at sexuality being used as a weapon of power.

In the early days of the community we had a number of discussions about whether or not we were excluding men. We are aware that we are engaging with a feminist way of being. On the whole women are comfortable with our style of community. We have a corporate sense of power, those in leadership try not to be authoritarian, we only have structures if they help us add clarity to what we are doing. As the community has grown, however, there has evolved an increasing balance across the genders. We find that men are quite comfortable with the bread-making scenario and we are watching that the balance of power does not swing too much in the other direction.

There are certain designated hours when men are not permitted on the premises and these are times when we work alongside female survivors of abuse. We are aware that there are also male survivors who have scant provision for their needs. At present we are not working with them, although some day we hope that this might be possible. However, for obvious reasons, when we are working explicitly alongside female survivors we ensure there are no men present.

The whole area of spirituality and mental health is a contentious one. While this subject is high priority on the health service agenda there are those health-care providers who treat it with suspicion. Undoubtedly spirituality and mental health issues are linked. In their book *The Spirit of the Child* (1998) David Hay and Rebecca Nye describe the spiritual experiences of a group of 38 children aged 6 to 11 years old. They discovered that almost all these children tended to use religious language to explain life, conscience, power and creation even if they had no affiliation with a religious community. The children were already 'aware that there is a social taboo on speaking about spirituality' (p. 104). Similarly 70 per cent of the population in the 2001 census described themselves as Christian and rejected the option to claim no faith at all. While many still talk of spiritual experiences there are clearly times when this spiritual dimension of our lives becomes unhealthy. This is often associated with bouts of poor mental health where the church can become a magnet for people's needs.

At Somewhere Else we have hit these issues in some quite close encounters. A manic depressive member of our community was so plausible that he was able to promise all kinds of things to people for whom that wish expressed their heart's desire. He had the ideal job for someone dissatisfied with their present employment. He had a cottage in the countryside for someone desperate for a holiday. In this instance we were brought up sharp but not quite soon enough. We try to give people the benefit of the doubt, to listen to stories and believe them. Sometimes illness can weave a web of virtual reality that is so plausible it is easier to believe than to doubt. We have learned a lot. We try to accept that often what people tell us is at best only partly true. If that partial reality begins to affect the most vulnerable among us then we are on our guard. This is a very difficult and sensitive area because we want to offer a place for people whose mental health issues have made them lonely and excluded. But sometimes it is impossible and we are sorry.

People who have been abused look exactly the same as anyone else. If you are an average churchgoer there will probably be half a dozen survivors (at least) in your congregation. In most churches we simply do not talk about it – sexuality is assumed to be private and should be kept under wraps. Abuse is not so much about sexuality but about power. Sometimes that power is exerted in sexual ways but often it is by physical or emotional violence or neglect. It is extremely difficult to disclose a history of abuse. It is hard to listen to, but it is always harder to tell. People who disclose abuse should always be believed and taken seriously. This listening needs wisdom and a very clear set of boundaries. One of the characteristics of abuse is that boundaries have been violated, and anyone who listens should set the parameters for appropriate contact. This is a mark of sound pastoral care.

One feature of endeavouring to provide a safe place at Somewhere Else has been that a number of survivors have felt able to tell their stories. I have been able to follow the path of one particular story and go with the person involved to places that evoked memories, which made it easier to connect with their personal history. This has been time-consuming and distressing but also a great privilege. The person involved has a great deal of wisdom about boundaries, and for this I am profoundly grateful because in effect I have been learning on the hoof. Most of us are unskilled in this area. I have had to swim way out of my depth but with a lot of supportive friendship and wisdom I have been able to travel an important road both with the survivor concerned and for myself. It has not been easy. Contact with CSSA (Christian Survivors of Sexual Abuse) has been a wonderful gift to our community. We have met not just 'survivors' but a remarkably resourceful set of very different human beings who have learned how to flourish despite abuse. We are now employing someone to work with survivors and alongside clergy as they learn best practice. At present this is a short-term contract but we hope to find funding to continue the work. The CTBI report *Time for Action* is a wonderfully sensitive and wise document and to be recommended.

Our community is small and that is to the good. We have an intensity of life experience and issues that take some holding. We are each needy of support and proper attention. We each need our own space. How foolish then to have created a church around a kitchen, traditionally the most contentious of church environments! We have at our heart a piece of communal territory that we must negotiate wisely. I suppose I am jaundiced from the five years in my previous appointment spent trying to free the church teaspoons from captivity. So at Somewhere Else we try to negotiate space. Sometimes we do this well and other times we mess it up big time. The art is in not always doing it right but knowing how to get yourself out of the mess when you are in it.

During the week, groups come and go from the rooms. Some groups choose to be anonymous, others are happy to mix. Gay and lesbian groups might want to remain confidential, as not everyone is 'out'. Survivors need a feeling of safety and also to know the whereabouts of exits. Some people need quiet, other people need to make a racket, some people need space, and others can squeeze in with everybody else. The negotiation of space is a time-consuming activity that sometimes needs the negotiating skills of an anti-hostage team. The basic skill, however, is to be able to say you are sorry when you get it wrong. How many church communities are living in silent opposition to each other because they can't negotiate their territory? We don't always get it right – but we do try to admit it when we get things wrong.

Don't panic? Well, at least don't let it show! All the above sets into motion a dynamic with a seemingly infinite number of variables. Random groups of people with overt and private issues, tendencies to react in certain ways in certain settings, people who might be economical with the truth or downright liars alongside the vulnerable and easily led. I sense we travel a narrow path at times. That is why we depend so much on each other's wisdom. And there is a great deal of wisdom in our community simply because it is so varied. The wisest person when it comes to issues of abuse is someone who knows what it is like to live through abuse. If you want to know what it feels like to be a transgendered person then ask Penny – she has a wealth of insights born out of her own experience.

That is why the quality of our conversation is so important. We need to trust each other. Sometimes this is very difficult because what is happening sets off all kinds of impulses within each of us. None of us is unaffected by the issues around. We can get very annoyed with each other at times. Sometimes we just get stuck. Col, of course, has the phrase here: 'We don't have to be good, we have to be real.' Some of the issues we face day by day are insoluble. However good a minister I am, I cannot undo the impact of sexual abuse, but I can be real about how it is for me and I can be genuine in the way I engage and try to listen. Honesty goes a long way.

Ultimately, of course, it is about trusting God amid the muddle. We may not be able to see a clear way through from beginning to end but there is graciousness in the way God is dealing with us. Grace is not about denial – it is about loving all of us, even the struggling parts.

Safe place?

We have tried to make Somewhere Else a safe place but it will never be so. Living is not safe. The very nature of the people we are and the encounters we experience will engender a dynamic that challenges each of us. There are, however, some practical things we can do to make this a 'safer place'.

One is to be aware of exits and entries. That is why at one recent faith sharing evening you would have found us taking it in turns to stand on the pavement and ring the doorbell. We are not 'open house' – people cannot just drift in from the street to be with us. We have a doorbell and an intercom system to let people in and out. At any one time we should know who is present on the premises and we are free not to let people in if we sense that it would make us or others vulnerable. We try to be sensitive to other people's difficulties on entry and exit. Some people can breeze into a room full of people without any difficulties, others like to be left alone while they acclimatize. Andrew comes straight into Somewhere Else from a very highly pressured office, and we know that we need to leave him quietly until he has unwound enough to be part of a group.

The 'code of respect' sets guidelines as to how we intend to be with each other. Not only does this give us some markers for our own behaviour, it also gives us permission to challenge others who might overstep the mark. Challenging inappropriate behaviour is really important but also very difficult. Churches are too often beleaguered by sulks and silences because members of a congregation have not challenged difficult behaviour. So, we do try to work things through as adults – and sometimes we succeed!

Another barrier to feeling integrated is the contentious matter of food. It has to be said that we are always eating but people should have choices as to what and when they eat. Some of our community have eating disorders or special needs. This is about helping each other not to feel under pressure or stuck. When we have space to be ourselves then we can start to grow.

Boundaries are different from barriers because we can set them in place ourselves. Rather than preventing people engaging with what is going on they set parameters for creative engagement. Any place of encounter needs to have clearly negotiated boundaries so that people know where they are. It is a false reality to say 'anything goes'. And it is more honest to name the boundaries than to assume that they are in place when they're not.

For all these reasons a community of people such as ours has a number of sharp edges. Not only do members come to places where their memories trigger emotional responses, we also encounter issues that knock us off balance. For instance, planning something as seemingly straightforward as a community vision weekend brings us to such practical matters as do all the room doors have a lock? Many retreat centres pride themselves on the fact that their remote location and Christian ethos means there is no need to lock bedroom doors, but this is of no use to a survivor who is feeling vulnerable. This sort of thing is actually an issue for all groups of people, because all groups of people, especially church groups, will contain survivors of abuse. It is only through knowing each other well enough to be able to voice such concerns and the willingness to take them seriously without prying that moves us into a discernment of good practice.

People can see difficulties as brick walls. I think this is too inorganic an image and prefer the image of 'hedges'. We often defend ourselves by growing prickly hedges. Everyone needs personal space and to protect it we find some sort of a screen, whether it be humour, bad temper, or holding back in some settings. If we are going to really see each other in a community we are better off with secateurs than battering rams. Gradually, as we learn to trust each other, we begin to name our needs and to claim our choices. We snip away at those defensive hedges. We do not try to uproot them but gradually they get thinner and some light shines through. We have permission to make our own boundaries. We don't need to make excuses for keeping some of ourselves for ourselves.

In this way we create slightly wider ledges to walk along. It may not be a completely safe place but it might be a safer place than most, especially if your life experience has been walking along precipices. There is room here for someone else to walk alongside you, maybe between you and the sharp drop. It's risky but it's real.

I sense that in all this it is our intentions that count. Yes, indeed, the road to hell is supposed to be paved with good intentions – but those are the ones that cause things not to happen out of our own neglect. If we intend the best for each other there is a demand put upon us to do our utmost to get it right. In this we are always destined to failure. Human nature and individual experience are so complex that with the best will in the world what we intend for good may be received otherwise. We experience this time and again at Somewhere Else. Even so, there is an inherent credibility in our desire to do good. We simply try and try again to take a loving path with other people in our sights. We try to apologize when things go pear-shaped and return to the endeavour with the benefit of hindsight. This is probably the area into which we put the most energy because it is about seeing people.

There is an African greeting which goes 'I see you'. This is not about eyesight but the inner eye that perceives a person to the depth of their humanity. When we are really seen we are understood, not summed up. We are allowed to be inconsistent and odd. We can be honoured for our difference and ambiguity. We try to do this as we work out what it means to be a community at Somewhere Else, not through some altruistic desire to please but simply because we believe God sees us.

How inclusive is inclusive?

The notion of inclusiveness has a certain political correctness about it. It is right and proper that all people of any racial origin, sexuality or ability are treated as equal human beings. I hope that goes without saying. It is however for this very reason that I believe there is a hint of paternalism about the notion of 'inclusiveness'. Who is including whom? In order to include someone there needs to be someone on the 'inside' doing the including. That someone, however altruistic they are, holds the power and sets the terms on which any inclusion is going to happen. There is an assumption that there is a place to be that is better or more to your good than the place in which you find yourself. There is an outsider, who can be welcomed by the insider who has something to give them.

James Alison in his book *On Being Liked* prompts us to think about the 'periphery'. He encourages us all to acknowledge our place on the periphery. The church is certainly no longer at the centre of society but maybe each of us as we recognize the eccentricity that God has given us, can benefit from acknowledging our peripheral dwelling. This is good news because it means we all have something to learn.

So, when Tony says, 'My Jesus is not your Jesus', he is not just making a statement about difference. He is saying that his insight is as valid as my insight, that there is room for a dialogue between us in which we can both hold equal power. In this dialogue, if we are brave enough to grasp it, lies a great hope. Those of us who sense our own vulnerability and insecurity are able to converse with each other about what matters to us. In this comes the possibility that we might be changed by another, might be made more complete or see another side of an argument.

We may never reach a place where we all agree (I hope not) but we will reach still points where we see others on the periphery to be companions on the road rather than antagonists in a battle. Companionship is about upholding each other even in the light of difference, acknowledging that our difference is a gift and the means of transformation both for ourselves and for the whole community.

We recognize that we often dwell in the micro-environment of individual encounter. This may lead to a false sense of security because when individuals encounter institutions this can be a less empowering experience. I am aware of this particularly with the gay and lesbian Christians who are so integral to our community that it is possible to be lulled into a false sense of security in relation to the wider church. Initially I provided the interface between the Somewhere Else community and the structures of the church. I went to a synod, I was the representative on the ecumenical team, I was the link person on the police liaison group, I negotiated the gay blessings with people in the church. I suppose I wanted to protect my community in their perceived vulnerability from institutions in their perceived powerfulness. I do not think this was a mistake. We have had to learn to trust each other and that has been fragile process. But now things are changing and this is because the community itself is changing them. Penny is a representative of the trans-gendered community on the Police forum, Carole and Hilary have both embarked on store chaplaincies under the auspices of the ecumenical team, Col has a job working with survivors and is chair of the national committee of the CSSA. Marie is liaising with the gay and lesbian forum of the Methodist Church. I consulted with a friend as to whether revealing all this in a book would be counterproductive, whether it would lead this community into a place of rejection. Certainly it is a risk. But I am now more confident that they are able to stand their ground. It seems that the attention to individual experience is building the confidence of the community in relation to structures. As my friend advised, 'The church needs to know about this other way of being – if you don't tell them, who would believe it?'

I see that my role in this community is changing and the encouraging and upholding task is being transformed into something else as the community claims its own power. This is undoubtedly good. Maybe soon the role of leadership will need different skills from the ones I can offer. That is also good. Shortly it will be time for me to move on. In the years before that happens I need to ensure one or two things. First, that there are the resources within Somewhere Else to help it resist the pressure to institutionalize itself. As Marie said, 'This is an uncomfortable place and the time to worry is when it becomes comfortable.' Second, there is a need for me to encourage the community to have enough confidence in itself to hold its head up when faced with structures that would seem to undermine it. There is a justifiable pride in being part of this community – not a conceited arrogance but a sense of belonging to something life-giving. It is important to be able to articulate this in constructive and gracious ways.

Gracious living isn't about a set of aspirations or middle-class norms. It is living believing that each day is a gift from God. It is about living generously, with an attitude of hospitality because that is how God has come to you. This is a fragile yet supremely strong perspective. It means being prepared to live with the assurance that whatever befalls us there is nothing that can separate us from the love of God in Christ Jesus. So we are free to live on the edge with all the struggle and insecurity that this implies. It is the gift of having nothing but God's love, it is a gift that comes when silence calls us by name.

When Steve came to Liverpool, his 'friend' stole his rucksack. He lost the few things he had brought with him, including his mobile phone with the numbers of everyone who mattered to him. He slept a few nights under a bush outside the Metropolitan Cathedral and when we met him he was on our doorstep selling the *Big Issue*. Steve came to sit with us, to eat and to make bread. After a few weeks he was helping to deliver the bread. He managed to find a place in the YMCA and enough confidence to ask if he could lead a Faith Sharing group. He is now so much part of this community that it is hard to remember a time when he wasn't around.

One day Steve called in unexpectedly. I was in the middle of a meeting and he apologized profusely. He was carrying a large bunch of flowers. 'For you, Barbara', he said. We don't really have a proper vase so we put them in a beer glass in the middle of the table. That is living graciously.

Checking it out

Hermeneutics are the circles people go round to work out whether things are genuine or not. Checking things out with reference to tradition, Scripture and reason is a time-tested way to remain accountable. Is what I am doing so off the planet that no one would recognize it to be authentically Christian? In working with this question we need to refer to other wisdom, from the written word and from the traditions of the church.

I suspect that on the whole hermeneutics go round more in spirals than in circles. As each generation brings new insights, not just in theology but in psychology, genetics and sociology, our understanding moves onwards and the process of checking things out remains crucial.

The Methodist tradition has a heritage of pragmatism. That is, we tend to work things out with our sights on the person standing directly in front of us. This sometimes leads us to the assumption that pastoral well-being always transcends doctrinal rulings. When pastoral concerns lead us to do something differently, then we need to check out with tradition and reason. For instance, my theological understanding leads me to believe that baptism is once and for all. After all, God's grace is an absolute gift to us, we do not earn it and there is nothing we can do in our lives to justify it. God is love and we are made in his likeness. God's gift to us is to love us truly and faithfully, even when we don't know it.

Penny had been baptized as someone else. She had lost her faith and her identity because she thought that God seemed to be playing cruel tricks on her. When she found who she was, she asked to be baptized and I agreed, although I am aware that there would be many who would disagree with this move. I have to trust that God sees our intentions and desires and that we occasionally overrule our logic and our inherited theologies in the interests of a greater love.

Salvation is not a comfortable word for me. On the whole I prefer to go for the themes around redemption. Redemption frees us from a sense of a privatized faith journey with its roots in Western individualism. I believe that God calls back the whole of creation. Redemption gives us positive images, like a father waiting for his prodigal son, welcoming, embracing, longing. Maybe I had too many over-earnest Christians praying for me at university and felt that the salvation theme got hijacked into a rather smug sense of being on the right side of an ideological fence.

So, I return to the concept of salvation with trepidation, and I do so via the psalms. I have returned to the psalms with some focus recently while being on sabbatical in the Derbyshire dales. Each morning I take my Bible up the hill at the back of Wensley village. Down the valley to the right is Matlock in the distance. The cows in the adjacent field munch rhythmically, a grey mist lifts off the fields and I feel a million miles from city centre Liverpool – but the psalmists are right there. With Col they are saying, 'We don't have to be right, we have to be real.' What they are most real about is their need of salvation.

The images we find in the psalms, however, are earthed and spoken from a sharp edge of humanity. As I sit on the hillside I read the psalm out loud: 'A herd of bulls surrounds me, strong bulls of Bashan close in on me; their jaws are agape for me like lions tearing and roaring' (Psalm 22.12). Suddenly I am not quite so comfortable, I hope those bullocks in the next field aren't listening! It goes on: 'For he has not despised or disdained the poor man in his poverty, has not hidden his face from him, but has answered him when he called.' And Psalm 18: 'I love you, Yahweh my strength (my saviour, you rescue me from violence). Yahweh is my rock and my bastion, my deliverer, is my God. I take shelter in him, my rock, my shield, my horn of salvation, my stronghold and my refuge.'

The psalmists are real flesh and blood people in fear of their lives and they are not so much interested in God saving them in some future realm beyond death as in giving them a safe place and a way out of trouble right now.

I don't think I am usually an angry person but I was incensed the day I found Rob, selling the *Issue* on our doorstep, being harangued by a passing vicar out shopping with his wife who had stopped to tell Rob that if he believed in the Lord Jesus he would not be homeless. I believe that for Rob, to be saved means to be safe, to be inside and warm and fed, not being preached to by a meandering parson.

Maybe you think this is selling out on the gospel? Well, maybe it is selling out on a middle-class gospel that implies we are all free to make choices. But when life undermines your physical and emotional safety then a shield and a stronghold are more immediately useful than a text and a promise. Well, that's my opinion anyway.

On Easter Sunday two guys turned up for a spot of lunch and some time out from being kicked. One of them had had his ear cut off in a fight and had a bandage right round his head. They ate and ate and slept and slept. The world went on around them. Later that day they were arrested and spent the rest of the holiday weekend in prison. It was the day of Penny's baptism and we had met early in the morning beside the Mersey for communion, using our own bread, before walking up the hill for that most wonderful service. Col was Godmother. At lunchtime we listened to ourselves on the radio – we featured in Radio 4's *Food Programme* – while we shared a meal that had appeared from various carrier bags around the room. All of this seemed unbelievable. Here was a little gospel community that had emerged from nowhere. There was a great sense of wonder.

I cannot explain to you how this is. Although I can tell you individual stories, the patchwork pieces that make up the emerging community, explaining it is beyond me. I think that ultimately this is how faith should be. That is not to say that we should be lazy about working things out; we should do our best to be able to speak our faith and make sense of it. We need to work through all the words before we reach the silence but ultimately it is a mystery. Faith is like music, dancing or the aroma of new-made bread –

one of the simplest and most profound things. As such it remains far beyond words.

Col's prayers for Easter Sunday

Lord we come before you knowing that we hurt each other and make mistakes. We are sorry.
Help us to let go of guilt.

Lord, we often put boundaries on your love and limit the lengths we think you will go to reach us.
Help us to feel your love.

You have asked us to love ourselves and the people who come into the labyrinth of our lives.
Help us when this command is particularly difficult.

The news each day is often hard to hear, of others who are drowning in wells of tears.
Help us to show empathy when it is easier to feel sorry for ourselves.

You gave life back to Lazarus' family. Help us when the losses in life are too hard to bear and show us the ways to let go and trust that all will be well.
Help us when the sky is dark and the sun is hidden by the clouds.

The truth will set you free, says our God who does show positive discrimination. You are loved unconditionally. You are invited every day to let go of the baggage which hinders your journey. I am on your side not against you.

Amen

4

Scarecrow Ministry

Being stuck in

In looking to be part of an emerging Christian community I have wanted to encourage you to live with the muddle and mystery of what will emerge. Wait and listen. Courage to live this process is costly. There will be times of confusion and uncertainty in which you will need all your wit and a set of trustworthy companions. There is a need to continue checking out its authenticity. Along with a great deal of delight there are dangers and pitfalls. We need to keep focused on our core agenda, listening out for echoes of the kingdom and looking for signs of salvation that are inclusive and loving. This is a courageous journey in which there are embedded some deep questions around leadership.

Over the last five years I have thought a lot about my ministry. The fact that I was appointed as a superintendent to a city centre circuit without a building or a congregation has caused this hard thinking. What does it mean to be a minister in this situation? How is ministry linked with mission? What kind of leadership is expected of someone with nothing visible to lead?

I was aware that a comment by a friend of mine referring to my work as a 'church plant' had provoked a defensive response from me. The notion of bringing to the city centre a predetermined idea about church and then imposing it on this particular space may be a caricature of church planting but it was one that contradicted what Somewhere Else is all about. I replied, 'I'm not planting a church, I feel more like a scarecrow!' Like a scarecrow I felt that my job was to watch and wait. To get stuck into a patch of soil without the first idea of what was going to emerge – if anything. This sort of ministry is much harder in some ways than coming to plant a church. It is easy enough now to look back and say, 'All we needed to do was wait, and look, a church occurred,' but that was far from the case at the beginning. We had no idea whether there would be a Christian community emerging from the bread-making enterprise or not. We never set the formation of a church as a core agenda – indeed it has come as somewhat of a surprise. All we felt called to do was to be present to our questions and to make bread.

Ministry has been formed by mission. A theology of mission that says God is ahead of us, active and alive even in the absence of church. It has set a pattern of searching ministry. If God is ahead of us then what is he up to? The scarecrow minister has no option but to be firmly rooted in the soil and wait and see. That means a depth of dogged faith that is prepared to stand firm despite all the evidence that God is absent.

Maybe one of the most distinct features of city centre work is that it has few clear boundaries. It may be easy enough to look on a map and describe the geography of a city centre but it would be an illusion to believe the place or the work is in any way contained by geography. Geography is nevertheless important and in Liverpool the main feature is the river. Most cities are circular in shape with the centre in the middle, skirted by inner-city areas and the suburbs on the edge. Liverpool is semi-circular with its centre on the river. Some might say that the other half of the city is to be found on Wirral but I am far too much of a coward to suggest it myself!

Along the Liverpool waterfront the architecture speaks of the history of the place. Dock Road, once the route for countless dockers travelling the overhead railway to queue for work, now leads to the container terminal where ships are now unloaded by crane. At the Pier Head are the 'Three Graces', a series of buildings whose architecture speaks of the dominance of shipping and the money associated with international trade. On the top of the Liver Building stands the mythical griffin, birds who are said to flap their wings if a virgin walks underneath! Further along the Albert Dock are cotton warehouses now refitted for the tourist and club scene and the museum of Liverpool Life with its memories of the slave trade.

Up the hill to the south of the city centre, joined by Hope Street, are the two cathedrals of Liverpool. These buildings offer distinctly different styles although both were completed in the twentieth century. Drawing the semi-circle, then, with an imaginary pin pushed in at the Pier Head and with the radius taking in the two cathedrals, is the geography of the city centre. Within this patch are contained three universities, retail developments, flats and houses, the Philharmonic Hall, theatres, countless clubs, pubs and restaurants, a business sector, law courts, police headquarters, charity shops, art galleries, council chambers – enterprises large and small of every description.

So, city centre work has a closely defined geography but its boundaries are permeable as huge waves of population shift during the course of each day. Not only does the population shift between day and night but also the types of people coming and going are also shifting. Cleaners and key-holders, shopworkers and secretaries, wanderers and pickpockets, judges and asylum seekers are all present on the same street. Trying to stand in solidarity with such a place is something like trying to hold a bubble – as soon as you get any sort of grip on it, it disappears. That's why it is impossible to talk of any sort of church model. It is impossible to model an open system that changes aspect every day. A scarecrow ministry is about standing in the not understanding.

As a scarecrow stands over an empty allotment so the ministry in those early days was about believing in the possibility of something as yet unknown. What happened was a lot of random encounters with all kinds of people all over the place. This process was quite bizarre. I met with the homeless guys, with other clergy, with the police, with office staff and shopworkers, with volunteers, with charity workers. These people simply emerged.

The temptation was to try to make sense of these encounters and to knock them into some sort of shape that gave them meaning. Like a scarecrow who doesn't know what crop has been sown on the patch, I simply tried to hold on to the randomness of these encounters, not trying to ascribe meaning to them but allowing them to be and either disappear or flourish. That is a hard agenda because it is tempting when we are lonely to try to bring meaning to what is happening to us. It was necessary to live with a lot of loneliness. Every day I was thankful to Donald, who lived the waiting time with me and encouraged me to desist from naming things too readily.

In this early time the minister holds an observer position. I watched and pondered, listened and wondered. It was important that I not only watched and listened but also wondered and pondered. The wondering and pondering of the observer position is a move away from voyeurism. For every week I spent in the city centre I took two or three days away from things to remember and reflect upon what I had actually seen and heard. Some of the things that continue to emerge are very tiny indeed. It is so easy to miss significant things because we are preoccupied with those things that present themselves most forcibly as important.

Scarecrow ministry is less about planting something and more about looking lovingly at an empty patch, hoping for signs of life, staying with the belief in the invisible things God has sown. So also the ministry of struggling churches is this lonely process of waiting and watching. I want to discourage an endless round of schemes and courses that will enliven our churches – the 'if only we had some young people' mentality. On the contrary, I encourage you to watch and wait, listen and reflect upon the question that God has given only to you.

Waiting

For those of us who are used to being led by agendas, waiting is the hardest thing. Standing and watching challenges not only our outward resolve but also our inward motivation. It is easy to become dispirited or uncertain about whether or not it is all worth it. That's why churches tend to leap into busy, task-centred ministries. There is no short cut in the process of watching and waiting. It is simply necessary to trust the process. If God is ahead then God will become visible. We must stand fast and believe in the not-yet-ness of things.

I found it particularly difficult because I am married to a minister who at that time had pastoral charge of five suburban and inner-city churches. You can imagine the dynamic at the tea table when he was on a fast turnround from day-time visits and paperwork to an evening meeting. What had I been doing all day? It's hard to answer 'watching and waiting' while those around us are driven by many agendas into a life of activity. Now I know that the year spent just being in the city was formative to everything that emerged after that. It set a pattern for being present that has enabled us to set the need for space, silence and reflection as key aspects to our bread-making community.

When groups of people are up to their elbows in sticky dough and there is noise and chaos all around us, we remember that God has always been ahead of us and that we must continue to trust the process of revelation and discernment. Watching and waiting will return us to the heart of the matter, to our dependence on a God who watches and waits with us and will continue to surprise us.

It helps us to be open to possibilities. One thing I try to practise is to say 'yes' without asking 'how?' When a possibility presents itself I try to see it as a gift and work with it. A group of students wanted to put on an art exhibition and they asked if they could use our rooms. I said 'yes, of course'. They used each of the rooms as an element: earth, air, fire and water. They had pictures and sculptures, photographs and models. One room was completely blacked out and had woodchips on the floor, one room was filled with feathers. They asked if they could paint clouds on boards and use them in the air room. I said 'yes, of course'. Then they said they couldn't get the boards up the stairs and could they paint the clouds on the walls if they promised to paint them away again. I said 'yes'. The clouds were so impressive that when the students left we asked if they would leave them for us. Our quiet room is now called 'the cloud room' as the sky outside matches the blue sky and white clouds on the walls. A group of students now have a positive image of the church, and we have a wonderful quiet room, just by saying 'yes'.

This is, of course, a risky process. The scarecrow's patch could simply be full of weeds. We could end up with a disparate and dysfunctional community with no sense of purpose or faith. I began to panic when two white witches turned up. This is where the 'scarecrow' has to trust the 'farmer'. This is not an empty patch of soil with nothing good in it. If we believe God is ahead of us we must trust in his goodness. This is not just an exercise in wishful thinking, however, it needs a great deal of dependence on his promises. We are diligent in our prayer, in reading the Scriptures and in working out the imperative to love one another. We do not wait in a vacuum but with a faith that has stood the test of time. We may be confused but we don't need to be afraid.

I have always been particularly struck by the words of the third Eucharistic prayer used in the Church of England's *Alternative Service Book*:

> Father we give you thanks and praise
> Through your beloved Son Jesus Christ ...
> He opened wide his arms for us on the
>   cross;
> And put an end to death by dying for us
> And revealed the resurrection by rising to
>   new life;
> So he fulfilled your will and won for you a
>   holy people.

The prayer puts together two key concepts in the shape of one image, the outstretched arms as a sign of acceptance and sacrifice, and the way in which new life can be claimed through Jesus.

I have worked within churches that considered themselves to be 'welcoming communities', but had not grasped that welcome and sacrifice are part of the same package. Church noticeboards that say 'Welcome to our church' give a signal that you are accepted if you are willing to comply with terms of entry – usually something about a protocol of acceptable behaviour. They speak of a powerful community rather than a sacrificial one.

Sacrificial welcome is a much deeper and holier concept. It is about meeting whoever God sends to the door in a way that we anticipate we would want to meet Jesus – and that is exceedingly costly and exceedingly demanding.

Andrew writes:

> *Somewhere Else is like an orchestra – it is constantly changing because of the make-up of the members – it can be light and frothy, dark and serious, whimsical or sombre, small or large, harmony or discord – God provides the notes – the mystery of it is that the players seem to be able to arrange the notes to bring music.*

The image of the scarecrow's wide open arms is one that demands a lot of energy. Living each day not knowing who will arrive and who will leave and giving permission for both to happen is a sacrificial call. At first it felt as if it was just me who was living this way and while I found unexpected arrivals challenging and surprising, the leaving was infinitely harder. Letting people arrive and depart became a rhythm of the place but it was and is never easy for me personally. So much of 'success' in ministry is seen as what or who you have gathered in, rather than a dynamic of human experience. It was necessary not only to learn to swim against the emotional flow but also to acknowledge the cost of such a process on my own inner resources.

Scaring away the big birds

There are all sorts of big birds that may gobble up tender shoots. The scarecrow's job is to see them coming and fend them off. This requires perceptiveness. These birds can come in many guises. Initially whole flocks came as negative emotions: 'This is not possible', 'You can't possibly do that', and then the more subtle ones, 'Well, it's quite a nice little project but when will it be a real church?' There were moves from other churches to come and plant congregations in the city centre because there was nothing particularly visible on my patch. The area looked like a vacuum waiting to be filled.

These emotional birds were insidious in their working. They made me doubt that I was in fact doing anything useful. Was the bread-making idea just a whim that would quickly pass? Plenty of people laughed at me, shrugged their shoulders or made sarcastic comments just out of earshot. Scaring away the big bird of my own self-doubt was one of the biggest challenges. I knew that we were operating in a realm of virtual reality where the vision was invisible to most. We had to state what was happening as if it was happening. I used to say, 'I have got a real church, you just can't see it yet!'

Another emotional big bird was that of loneliness. I knew that I couldn't rush into gathering people around me, but it was difficult to hang on to the solitude. Most ministers live with a huge amount of loneliness despite the people who flock around them. We are present but we never quite belong. Solitude brings gifts but it also brings dangers, such as sinking into depression or laziness. On the other hand, it is possible to go into overdrive in an attempt to prove our own worth. We can be fraught with self-doubt or cling on to dubious certainties.

A joke during that first year went, 'Whose turn is it to take Barbara out for lunch today?' It was vital to have friends, friends who could question and sustain the lonely experience of the city centre. It was also necessary to live the loneliness. While I did in fact eat more meals out than was good for my waistline I also had to persevere with the isolation of what the city meant. There was no short cut to experiencing the city in all its variety and alienation. It is necessary to scare off not only the big bird of isolation but also the big bird of continuous company.

Big birds also come in many different people shapes. This has been a hard job for the scarecrow. How is it possible to be inclusive and welcoming, while at the same time chasing away those people who may cause others harm? Sometimes the most difficult people to scare away are other Christians. This may sound rather bizarre but some of the most awkward people to deal with have been other Christians who come assuming that they hold the power. They may be clergy who assume authority due to the position they hold within the churches or they might be Christians who are loaded with certainties. My alarm antennae are usually activated by the use of the words 'they' or 'them'. When someone refers to 'them', they are assuming there is an 'us' differentiated in some value-laden way. During Lent one year we were talking about survivors of abuse and a woman said, 'It's a terrible thing they have to face up to. How do you help them?' Among the group around the table, as in any church group, were a number of survivors. Not 'them' but 'us'. Challenging the 'them and us' mentality is tricky because it can be seen to be rude. We need to break through the categories that are so easily used as labels and honour the depth and wonder of human beings in all their diversity.

Bishops can be big birds. They may come in all humility and gentleness and we can be unguarded enough to make special arrangements. We can favour those people with influence and power simply because we are in the habit of doing so. Television companies can be big birds. We made a small piece for *Songs of Praise* and I was very aware that the next day there was going to be a gathering for survivors of abuse, none of the participants in which would want to be within a million miles of a TV station. So if the BBC needed to come back the following day to finish filming, we would have to say 'no' to them. That is easier said than done, as some people are not accustomed to being refused.

Then there is the big bird of success. The church, as with most of present society, tends to value success in measurable, numerical terms. 'Is our church growing?' It's a trend that's hard to resist. After a year I boasted to the synod that I had the fastest-growing church in the Liverpool district – we had gone from zero to three members. Everyone laughed but I knew that was a more significant growth than most. Funding bids on the whole ask for quantitative rather than qualitative assessment criteria. Talking the jargon that the funders require while not selling your soul to their means of assessing outcomes is an art form in itself.

There is the big bird of feeling good. While this shouldn't be disparaged, neither is it to be relished to the point of pride. It is always necessary to put in place mechanisms of accountability that guard against the temptation to indulge in a huge ego trip. These mechanisms can also be the safety net against despair. The emotional roller-coaster of a project such as this can test the most resilient of dispositions. No one should operate without a proper means of accountability.

So the scarecrow needs an abundance of discernment and wisdom. At Somewhere Else this was initially down to me, but as the community has developed so the bank of discernment and wisdom has also grown, thank God. There is a mutual accountability that is crucial. No one will do something on the say-so of someone with perceived authority. We are a rigorously questioning community and that has to be healthy.

Being ridiculous

Sam doesn't speak much English. Someone had teasingly referred to someone else as 'mad'. 'What is this "mad"?' asked Sam. Someone tried to explain. He thought about it for quite some time and then the penny dropped, 'Aha,' he said, 'then Barbara is double mad!' Well, it's no wonder Sam thought Barbara is 'double mad'. When he came to us he had been looking for a community in which to say his prayers. He had tried the Roman Catholics but did not find them particularly welcoming. He then wandered into the Jehovah's Witnesses and got confused. When he came to us and explained in his limited English what he was looking for I took a very deep breath before telling him that 'in this church we make bread'!

One of the features of the scarecrow is that it is dressed in a random selection of odd clothes, a discarded hat, a couple of odd gloves, a tatty old coat with a moth-eaten scarf. It is an object of ridicule. So too the bread ministry. We have had to live with being at best eccentric and at worst incomprehensible. We have had to be prepared to fit in with neither church nor secular expectations. We have had to tread our own path.

Over and over again I explain to people that we are a church and we make bread. It seems so normal to us now that we can hardly recollect the times when we had to explain who we were to complete strangers with nothing to show for the enterprise. It was at the beginning such a ridiculous notion.

As the years have gone by we consider 'bread church' to be normal and other churches to be bizarre, but we do acknowledge that we have in our community a quite ridiculous mix of humanity. Holding such an eclectic gathering takes some delicate facilitation. The people around the bread-making table would for no other conceivable reason be together in the same room. We meet in our humanity, in our common task of making bread, and in our intention to respect each other. It is a huge challenge, and each day brings a different set of people, a different set of circumstances, a different need to encounter.

Holding the unconnected nature of those who come to be with us can tax even the naturally patient. The community takes on a life that seems to spin. By that I mean that a small input or change can make a huge difference to the overall sense of well-being of the gathering. We live with a lot of apparent chaos and believe that the bread-making somehow works to bring people together. There is often a feeling of being out of control. We are usually exhausted by the end of the morning as we endeavour to welcome the unexpected, the surprising and the downright odd.

I am aware that this process has pushed my ministry into an area where I fit into neither current secular life nor the expectations of the church. I still attend the synod and other clergy meetings but my agenda varies hugely from those of my colleagues. I have begun to see things in completely different ways and to set different values upon what others consider norms. It has pushed me into a wonderful place but it is also at times excruciatingly lonely. Colleagues are often jealous – 'It's easy for you, Barbara' – or don't understand – 'Don't you miss your pastoral work, Barbara?' I am asked to talk about my work but sometimes sense there is an unhealthy curiosity about the request. 'You are doing a good job, Barbara, but it's not like that for us here, we don't have those sorts of problems here.' So often churches view society through monochrome spectacles. There is a huge wonder in the diversity around us, but we need to claim its oddness as a gift rather than a threat.

Marie says, 'We mustn't close the gap.' By this she means that it is right that our church is an uncomfortable place to be. When we start to feel comfortable, then we should begin to worry. We have huge challenges that appear from day to day. What should we do when one member of our community sits in my office and answers the phone? What should we do when someone with mental health issues is offering people holidays in a mythical cottage in Wales? How do we react when a lonely person so dominates a worship time that everyone else feels too uncomfortable to speak?

We struggle hugely with how to be accepting and loving without being naive or hurtful. We agonize over seemingly small things because they have triggered in us our own insecurities. We try to say that we honour difference but need to be real about the struggle to hold difference in creative ways. We try not to close the gap. In all this we may seem to be very odd. We will not answer these dilemmas in conventional ways. We struggle with our need to be nourished alongside our desire to be inclusive. If we appear to be 'double mad', then so be it.

This brings us to question the role of the minister. I am both part of this eclectic gathering and a stranger. I am as much a misfit in my own community as everyone else. There is such a diversity of experience and personality that I will never be someone who represents a 'norm'. I must be both rigorously professional and warmly involved. At a recent weekend away I was the only person present who was heterosexual. We often have groups in which all participants are survivors of abuse. Sometimes the majority of those present are homeless guys. Increasingly I am most uncomfortable when we have groups of middle-aged, middle-class church people at Somewhere Else. I no longer fit into any neat category, and I cannot close the gap between myself and my work. This is a challenge and a delight but it can also be confusing and isolating. I am a very oddly dressed scarecrow!

Being dismantled

An important aspect of scarecrow ministry is that the scarecrow will not be there for ever. There is a great temptation in a project such as the bread church to want to take root. After five years of hard work I am enjoying this community and the sense of growth and flourishing that I can now see. Tender shoots have now taken root. There are signs of people claiming their identity and thriving. The big birds are no longer so predatory. There are fruits to be seen.

All ministers must remember that this is God's story, not ours. The unfolding of the bread church has to be disengaged from the story of Barbara. This place now has a life of its own and must be free to grow in new directions. This is good, but it is not easy for me. Not that you need start applying for my job just yet! I'm here for a bit longer, but not for ever.

Ministry has in its job description a sense of bereavement. As Methodist ministers we are always moving on. This is both healthy and difficult. It seems that we are frequently asked to dismantle our lives and start again. I am not sure how I will move on from here but one day I must. Believing that this is God's story is helpful – there is part of my story that is not contained in this bread church thing. My own story will take different forms and move me to new places. This community has a new life yet to be discovered.

Maybe it is better to think of the scarecrow being recycled rather than dismantled. In the process of moving on I need to remember the essence of who I am in relationship to the God who calls me. This will need time for reflection and re-creation. Similarly, the community of Somewhere Else must learn to weather loss and find the essence of who it is becoming. As part of God's story there will be twists and turns in this experience for both of us. There are many uncertainties, but this is for sure – the farmer does not want to harvest the crop with a scarecrow in the way.

Casting the shadow of the cross

There was an argument about leadership in the emerging church in Corinth. Paul was getting irritated by the squabble. He says, 'I planted the seed and Apollos watered it but God made it grow. So neither he who plants or he who waters is anything but only God who makes things grow' (1 Corinthians 3.6).

Scarecrow ministry is only a means for the seeds to grow. When the seeds have taken root and are growing then the scarecrow has done its job. All ministry is about facilitating God's work, participating in God's story, nurturing God's people. The job of the minister is to remind us that we are part of this enterprise – just a small part.

There is the need always for the scarecrow to be casting the shadow of the cross. The shadow the cross throws is that of a person outstretched in love and suffering. This is God's story. Ministry is about embodying that story for a while and enabling the message of the gospel to overshadow a tender community. It is about endeavouring to live out the struggle between love and suffering and to speak of a hope that the tortured arms outstretched are also arms of welcome.

5

Transforming Stories

Story

As I began the story of 'Somewhere Else' I was aware that this was in essence 'my story', the story of how I landed in the city centre and what that experience did to me. As this narrative has progressed so other stories have been woven into the account. Cameos, snippets, testimonies or poems have all brought a diverse range and depth to the narrative that has unfolded. As these voices have emerged they have brought with them new challenges and questions. Along with all this has been the intertwining of Gospel stories, reminiscences and reflections, the theology and struggle of earlier Christians who in their turn lived out lives in the light of the resurrection of Jesus. It is as though, throughout time, we weave in and out of each other's stories.

There are, of course, parts of our story that we choose not to disclose. We keep some of our histories private, either because we consider them confidential or because we have not yet told them to ourselves. The accounts we tell of our childhood are refashioned in the wake of subsequent experiences. On the whole we put things in different perspectives as we get older. We move through and on from those past experiences. Sometimes they may trap us and we are stuck with unresolved issues that colour all subsequent encounters. Our memories are selective. We give weight to some parts of our history and forget others. We tell and retell our stories and they change in the telling.

This is also true of the Gospel writers. Each writes with his own slant and wonder. Each wants to draw out of his meeting with Jesus some sense of a bigger history. There are differences between the accounts, in their order and their content, adding new understanding to those early stories. Meeting Jesus in their own life stories caused those followers to communicate the impact it had on them, that it made such a subjective and eternal difference. Out of these Gospel narratives came an influence on society. People noticed the Christians. They were relating to each other with the imperative of a different way. It was something that impressed others. In time it began to shape society, politics and law.

On the day of Sam's baptism we held a small service at Somewhere Else and then walked up the hill to the Anglican cathedral. The building was full of people – there had been a deanery gathering from elsewhere in the diocese and there was the usual array of tourists and other visitors. We felt very small and insignificant. There were 12 of us and we gathered around the huge font that stands on steps at the side of the cathedral nave. We had a large jug of water, a small order of service, and our usual random selection of humanity.

When we returned to Somewhere Else there were 13 people. A Chinese student studying at the university and visiting the cathedral for the first time had joined us. She was a delightful young woman and talked freely about her studies and her family. When it came time for us to disperse she said, 'Thank you very much. I have never met Christians before but my friend told me that they are people who try to love each other. I can see that is true.' (You couldn't script it really!)

So we find time and again that this simple bread-making community has an influence far out of proportion to its size. We have friends in Cologne who want to set up a computer project with us. We have had visitors from the Anglican Lutheran society and a German visitor from Hamburg who came via Birmingham University. There is a continuing stream of students on placement from theological colleges and from local theology departments. We haven't been visited by an archbishop yet but we've had just about every other variety of clergy including a very special hermit who came each week to say his prayers.

This is all very well, but we are not a tourist attraction. If we are to remain faithful to who we are called to be then we have to continue to revisit our core story – we are called to be here and to make bread. It is very easy to be distracted.

One of the features of transformation is that we begin to change the story we tell. Revisiting memories or perhaps going there for the first time can be a hugely challenging process. Often it is triggered by the simple gathering of making bread. When our stories emerge we need someone beside us who will recognize the significance of the moment and listen our words into speech. That person needs not only to hear what is spoken but also to wait with us in the silences. They need to be able to uphold the process, letting the story find a way out and waiting with the parts that are not ready to be revealed. This is not counselling – we are quite clear that if people want to explore issues deeply then we will help them find someone with the time and skill to enable them to do so. I suppose what we offer is a solidarity best described as friendship or companionship.

Being a friend is different from being friendly. Companions know us within our stories. They are prepared to let us tell things over and over. Maybe most significantly they are willing to be changed by what we disclose. One mark of a church's attitude towards openness is how prepared it is to be changed by what it hears. That is not to say our opinions should swing from one extreme to the other in the light of one particular individual, but we should allow stories to question us. We are then prepared to live with the questions that emerge and not push them to closure. I sense that a mature community is one that begins to ask the right questions.

Through prayer and discernment we become part of the gospel story and in turn the gospel story begins to form who we are becoming. I believe this is what Jesus was doing with bread on the night he died. He was giving his followers the words of a true story – a story that would come back to them every time they broke bread from then on. 'Do you remember, on the night in which I died ... I took bread and broke it and gave it to you, saying, "This is my body broken for you, always do this when you break bread so that you remember me"?' I am sure that in their conversations in the early years after Jesus left them the disciples would remember that night each from their own perspective: 'I was pretty sceptical about it at the time', says Thomas. 'Me too,' says Peter, 'and I went on to make everything worse.'

One very wonderful experience happened last Easter. After words of institution, each person was invited to share bread with their neighbour in their own words. There was an initial hesitation, followed by a babble of voices. 'I made this bread and I want to share it with you because...', 'I am feeling fragile today and this crumbly bread reminds me of other people who are struggling today ...', 'This bread is for you because Jesus suffered and was homeless and he had friends like us ...'. So, the incarnate God becomes remembered as he enters our story and we are transformed in the connection.

Who will keep the story? Keeping a story is different from owning a story. Listening to someone else's story doesn't give us broadcasting rights. We must value confidentiality and trust. Telling our own story is part of what it means for us to be a human being, but to take someone else's story and use it for our own ends is robbery. Yet there is an essence of a story for our emerging community that, while it should never be set in stone, is also too good to be lost. Any story is as movable and as variable as the individuals who make it.

Similarly the Gospel story, with all its diversity and cultural baggage, is not ours to manipulate in order to make our own point of view irrefutable. One of the many wonders of biblical text is that it remains unchanging and sure while at the same time raising new questions. It continues to bring unexpected insights for different people in different places throughout history. We need to honour its wonder and steadfast assurance while still struggling with its challenges and conundrums.

Then there is the great story of the church. For 2,000 years faithful followers of Jesus have lived out their own stories in the light of the gospel. They have been prepared for that encounter to make a difference both to their individual lives and to the context in which they live. This has brought wonder and grace. It has also brought war, destruction and bigotry. We, like all Christians before us, are signed up for the struggle. We are still trying to get to the essence of the Jesus story. In this struggle there is always a need for more wisdom than any individual possesses. The history of the church is both an encouragement and a stark reminder of the divine imperative to be true to our roots in God as Father and Jesus Christ as Lord. And when we get it wrong there is the ongoing challenge of believing that God continues to love and forgive us as we begin again.

I suppose this is why I go on believing in the church. On our own we might manufacture a more custom-built manifestation of faith, but to whom are we accountable? How will we check out if our particular bright idea is the will of God or our own ego trip cloaked in ecclesiastical language? You only have to speak to a survivor of abuse whose pastor told her that to be healed she should have sex with him to realize that the wiles of satanic influence can come disguised as good intentions.

So the story is not to be held only by the powerful and the articulate. The story of the gospel is everyone's story and needs to be shared like the bread. Eucharistic bread is not owned by priests and preachers but is the bread of all creation. It is the body of Jesus, always mysterious and always empowering to the most vulnerable so that their story will be the primary influence for the church. The whole Christian community is the story keeper – here and now at Somewhere Else, throughout the Christian world and back in history to Jesus who said to that odd bunch of followers, 'Remember me.'

In the first year of wandering around the city I tried to know the *Big Issue* vendors by name. This is an almost impossible task because they come and go so frequently and are often found selling the *Issue* in a completely different part of town. I used to feel bad if I rounded a corner and met someone I knew but whose name had vanished from my memory. In order to help myself to not be so preoccupied with trying to remember that I wasn't concentrating on the conversation I was having, I would say inside my head, 'I can't remember your name so I will think of you as Jesus.' It sounds rather contrived but usually it relieved my anxiety long enough for me to be reminded of the guy's name and resolve to do better next time. Despite all contraindications I am in fact quite a shy person and find it difficult to talk with strangers.

After a while this ceased to be a memory game and began to form my theology. It helped me to realize that God was in fact ahead of me – not in some metaphysical spirit sense, but embodied in human form and in my vision. Now this has to be treated with some care. The person in front of me might be a Muslim or an atheist and be extremely offended by any assumption on my part, albeit unspoken, that they were somehow representing Jesus. Yet there is some essential truth here. That is, if I see you lovingly, then I will catch a glimpse of a divine spark in you. I will honour you because I recognize the divine story in you.

This sometimes happens the other way around in my retail chaplaincies. Wandering around a big city centre store wearing a dog collar and announcing that you are the chaplain has a mixed effect. Some people will be polite but have few words, some people will tell you their life story in every detail, others will have urgent business in the stock room. I am a very bad store chaplain. Even though I have the permission of the management to be there I find it incredibly hard to walk the stores. I don't visit as often as I should and every time it feels like starting again. It was a year before I had a sensible encounter with anyone and when it happened it was straight in at the deep end. I knew then that I had earned my credentials.

Earning my credentials partly came about when I gained a level of trust with one particular member of staff. She felt able to disclose a serious issue she was experiencing at home that was impinging on her work. I think that trust was earned by my trying to be nothing else but a genuine human being. I was helped to be genuine by overcoming my shyness by focusing on other people. This focus was helped to be God-centred by my saying to myself as I greeted people, 'I see the divine story in you.'

Recognizing the divinity of each other's stories is both life-giving to the churches and enhancing to faith outside the church box. If God is around then we will indeed, from time to time, catch a glimpse of him in each other's faces.

How do we learn to dance?

I have thought a lot about bread over the last five years. I have learned the practical skill of baking and come to value good ingredients. I have had conversations with bakers and acquired recipe books. I have learned about oil and yeast, salt and honey, how these basic commodities can bring something more than themselves. I have seen this transformation reflected in the people around me, in my community and in myself. All this thinking has given me a good story to tell – but it hasn't taught me to dance. Sometimes I have been stuck, worn out or downright grumpy (ask my children). It's like having the lyrics of a song but searching for a tune. I can hum it but who can play it?

Two things have connected in my head over recent months. One came about because a student who was writing her final year dissertation was trying to work out whether or not Somewhere Else was a genuine eucharistic community. She rang me up one day out of the blue with the question, 'Where is the wine, Barbara? I can get my head around the bread but where is the wine?' Several weeks later I was preparing to go on sabbatical when I found a retreat in a book entitled, 'The wine is the dancing'.

Eucharist is not only about bread, baked and broken. It is not only about fragile human beings returning to God and finding acceptance and life. It is, of course, about both these things but it is also about thankfulness. One wonderful feature of this little community is that it is at the same time both profoundly deep and profoundly funny. We hit some of the most difficult issues that prevail in our society – abuse, debt, homelessness, prostitution, isolation, fear. We hit them regularly and deeply and they consistently throw us off balance. We face them and return to them, we get it wrong, we apologize, we start again, we get irritated with each other and yet we continue to be friends. And without skirting around any of this we have a ball!

Take, for instance, the Somewhere Else Pantioke. This was a cross between a pantomime and karaoke and like all good pantomimes it happened in June. It featured Col as the Vicar of Dibley and yours truly had a bit part singing 'You can make me wholemeal again'. To that gathering came all sorts. Friends from work were invited along, Col's driving instructor, teenage offspring of various people associated with the community, and Ebbie the dog. Out of this random mix of humanity came not only a pretty wild night out but genuine interest in this bread church thing. No one knew church could be this much fun.

I secretly knew that in order for this to happen, someone was overcoming their claustrophobia, someone else had taken dancing lessons, a friend of someone else had offered the sound equipment for free, and so it went on. A visiting student was horrified that we were engaged in a social gathering of this sort at a secular venue without mentioning God by name. Yet we knew that God was intimately involved in our pantioke night. There are some significant people who are now members of our community who began to see on that night that it is possible to be a Christian and a real human being.

Being thankful isn't just something that happens in your head. It is about our whole bodies beginning to dance, to be able to be free enough from our hurts and histories to let our lives bubble up. That is not to deny that what has happened has happened by engaging in some meaningless distraction. It is about finding enough deep trust between ourselves to have fun, laugh and sing without fear. It is about rejoicing in our embodied humanity and saying, 'It is good to be here and alive and together with God and each other.' That's Eucharist.

Holiness?

I have been wondering a lot about holiness. It is, after all, supposed to be a mark of the church and its people. The holy people of God are distinguished by their likeness in some way to the holy God who has created them and sustains them. There is something essential of God that is reflected in the people who follow him but what it is that distinguishes them is sometimes elusive. People have spent their lives in search of holiness, lived in confinement or up poles. People like John Wesley were on such a quest and for him it led to the experience of his heart being 'strangely warmed'. Holiness is an elusive quality, maybe only distinguishable by God yet it is an important hallmark of the church. If what is emerging in Liverpool city centre around the bread is in fact an authentic Christian community then it should have the fragrance of holiness around it.

Holiness is a word that struggles to assert itself as it is so often aligned with the concept of perfection. In this postmodern world we may sense that we have broken free from some of our inherited concept of progress. Yet it is deep-rooted in our understanding of the world: 'Day by day in every way I am getting better and better.' Churches talk of 'pilgrimage', 'journey', 'discipleship', all concepts overlaid with the notion of spiritual progress, as if we are on a path towards completeness, a journey where there is some prospect of arriving in a state more acceptable and complete. This, of course, is not without biblical precedent.

For myself, and for the people of Somewhere Else, life has no prospect of being complete. Many of the things that have formed us have not only made us fragile but have also shaped us in ways where we sense there is no way back. No one ever recovers from abuse. No one with severe mental health issues will ever be free from the scars. And there is Donald with his troublesome back, which means his ministry must unfold from a sedentary position. I have come to know many holy people over the last five years, but none of us has in any way aspired to any sort of perfection.

Is being holy about being whole? What sort of wholeness does God offer us?

My hunch is that we have wrongly aligned a concept of being holy with both individualism and being complete. We have expected too little from our soul's journey. It is true that we are individual but that is not in an autonomous, powerful way. We are individual and that at its heart means we are fundamentally alone. We are born alone, we will die alone. Whoever accompanies us, our life's journey is a lonely one. To turn this essential loneliness into some kind of individual quest for wholeness is, in my opinion, to underestimate the depth of the spiritual journey. At the heart of who we are is a silence so deep that we will not begin to live until we have seen the dark centre of ourselves and known the echoes of silence it brings to us. Until we have known our own fragility and vulnerability we will not be touched by God who is in his essence fragile and silent.

Our hope in this profoundly lonely journey lies not so much in an individual effort to live another way but in the encounter with other people on the edge of the same dark, silent place. This connection has come to us through the bread-making. It is such a simple process, yet it gives the opportunity to talk of the deepest things at the core of our lives. It has become a means of enabling encounters that are safe, silent and deep, where the words at the very centre of our beings can come to the surface and can be honoured lovingly. When someone sees to the heart of our struggle, then we begin to say, 'This is who I am,' and we know we are accompanied in our isolation. Such accompaniment is the heart of how God is with us. Not the solidarity of completeness but of love's longing for life.

There is a wholesome aspect to this activity that is not about some abstract concept of wholesome living fraught with prohibitions. Our bread is good bread. It is made from the best of things. Ingredients are simple. We always have fresh fruit and vegetables. We sit together around a table, eating from proper plates and drinking fresh water from glasses. This is what many of us would expect if we were at home. Church has a tendency to cut corners and go for the cheap orange squash and plastic spoon option. If you are homeless, to sit around a table to eat in this fashion is a respite from a chaotic lifestyle. We say with simple hospitality more than many pious words could ever convey.

It is also wholesome to treat people with courtesy and gentleness. To care about how they are welcomed and to see each as an individual with special needs for safety and space. There is an aspect of holiness in this simple way of being with each other. It brings equality to the heart of the community. Respect is at the core of how we are day to day with each other.

From this emerges a wholesome laughter and lightness of spirit.

There is something about holiness that has a physical priority. We are embodied human beings. What we eat and how we eat it matters to our sense of well-being. Our bodies and our souls are not separate entities; they can't live separate lives. They are both an integral part of who we are. If we are hungry and unsettled, how can we pray? If we have slept under a bush for three nights, how can we make friends?

This is not simply an individual need but the need for any community. Sometimes church caterers provide the finest of meals but at the expense of a sense of belonging. At one church known to me a new member was so scolded for chopping the tomatoes in the wrong shape that she vowed never to return to the kitchen. Wholesome living is also about gracious living. Giving each other room to be ourselves. Giving each other the benefit of the doubt. Negotiating where the power lies.

Holistic therapies aim to bring health by looking at the whole of the person. They acknowledge that well-being isn't simply about being healed. In fact, our overall health may have little to do with alleviating symptoms of a particular complaint. Body, mind and spirit need to have some integrity if we are to reach our full potential as fulfilled human beings. Christianity has had a tendency to be body-denying – the things of the spirit are given greater weight than the physical matter around us. We sometimes lose sight of the fact that one of the authors of Genesis describes God fashioning us out of the red earth, breathing life into us and giving us form.

In reminding us of our link with the soil, the bread-making brings to mind our dependence on the physicality of the earth that sustains our physical bodies. Unless all of us are nourished we will not thrive. Our bodies need food as much as our minds need ideas and our spirits need a sense of wonder and grace.

I think the bread church offers a wider understanding of holistic than simply that of individual integrity. This wider understanding brings to light that holiness is about community. As the diverse gathering convenes to make bread there is a sense in which our very diversity adds to each other's wholeness. Because we are together, because we share stories and because those stories have the potential for changing all of us, then we each become richer and deeper. Such mutuality means that our individual journey becomes less important than our community reciprocity. We each flourish as all flourish, we all flourish as each flourishes. The 'holistic' idea may be a concept that inspires people to explore an individual spirituality. I sense holiness is more about an integrated understanding of what it means to be individuals together.

If I had to describe my ministry in a nutshell I would use the word 'holding'. I sense that for the last five years I have 'held on'. I have held on to a vision and then to the people who have come to be part of that vision. Sometimes I have had to hold on even though there was very little visible and people were scathing or indifferent. I have had to hold on to my own sense of being. Like most ministers I have needed to go on believing in people when they have let me down. I have had to hold on to God even when he seemed elusive or downright annoying.

In saying this I am also aware that there has been much that has needed to be ungrasped. It has been necessary to let go of certain learned behaviour. I have had to risk being changed as the experience and the stories associated with Somewhere Else have begun to shape the community. Most painfully, I have had to let go of people who were called elsewhere to live their lives in a different context.

I want to use the concept of 'holding' with some care. I believe Somewhere Else is a place of holding people that are in transition but it is not a place of entrapment. People are always free to leave, always able to move on, always able to disagree and opt out. Maybe in the light of this the better word is 'upholding'. We are a community that seeks to uphold people who may be confused or wounded. We cannot fix life experience but we can give space and attention. We can simply offer people a breather while they work it out.

We want to uphold people in this way because of a growing belief in the way God is with us. I know that none of this would have been possible but for the God who has held on to me. How preposterous to think that I am holding on to God; rather, each day of my life is upheld by the one who holds underneath me his everlasting arms. God is not a grasping taskmaster who expects us to live up to certain standards or fear the consequences. On the contrary, he sees our fragility and struggle and at the moment we start sinking upholds us. So holiness is more than the holding of one individual by another. Holiness has something of the steadfast undergirding of God's faithfulness as we work out what it means to be a community in the palm of his open hand.

So I return to an understanding of holiness that is essentially the nature of God. God is holy. No one has the full picture, though we may sometimes catch a glimpse reflected in the eye of someone in passing or in an encounter along the way. I have come to a place where I see that holiness is not so much a state of arrival but a way of being. It is the way of being with each other that most reflects God's way of being with us. I see that God's way of being with us as bread-makers has been to bring integrity to our faith community. We try to incorporate every aspect of ourselves and every aspect of each individual who forms the community. Those many parts are complex, damaged, wonderful and troubled. We are all these things. We are like the deepest of rivers, always changing, sometimes turbulent, deep, frightening and beautiful. A place in which to be refreshed, to splash on the surface or to explore new depths.

If the church is to grow in holiness then there is a need to see the richness of the whole of God's creation. The earth and everything in it is holy and that means we are challenged to live with diversity. Whatever veneer we adopt we will never be a monochrome society. The poor are always with us, as are the frantic, the disjointed and the confused. We are all these things in our turn. We each need space to be upheld and cherished. This is our deepest challenge: to live out our own complexity and to treasure the complexity of others in such a way that the essence of God's love can soak into our souls.

I am the bread

So much of the Christian's self-understanding comes with the language of the journey: 'pilgrimage', 'walking the faith'. Over the last five years I have come to value a different motif – the call to abide in God's love. Paul challenges the people of Thessalonica to 'hold fast to that which is good' (1 Thessalonians 5.21). These images come not from a sedentary existence but rather from the turbulence of building a Christian community in the context of upheaval and questions. If we are to hold fast to that which is good we must be people who hone all our skills and insights in order to discern what is good.

Then we must be prepared to go for it, whatever the distractions and pitfalls. It may be the image of clinging to wreckage in a rough sea or to the hand of a guide in a crowded street rather than that of an intrepid pilgrim trekking off towards the promised land.

I find this 'holding fast' imagery to be useful because it gives us both rest and commitment. It gives us rest because it is not down to us to strive towards some notion of perfection. We are not off to search for the Holy Grail, as if it belongs in a land we do not know. The place of encounter with God is right here, in our bread-making, in our city, in our friendships and in our silence. God is asking not that we go in search of him but rather that we recognize that he is already with us. God upholds us here and now, even in these muddled times, even in our half-belief, even when we get it so completely wrong.

At the same time as being given rest, we are stirred up to be more committed. As a minister I have often read rather ruefully the passages in the Gospels, 'Come to me all you who are weary and heavy laden and I will give you rest.' It seems that God has never given me much rest: commitment has meant activity, activity has meant energy spent trying to live a faithful life, and energy spent has often meant exhaustion. We can so easily mix up commitment with activity. We sign newcomers up for jobs in church so that they will feel they belong and very quickly they can feel trapped and exhausted. The bread church has helped me to be less concerned about commitment and more concerned about being present. When we are present to each other, deeply and attentively, then there is an amazing emergence of a sense of belonging.

We belong because we feel not only that the community upholds us but also that God upholds us.

This is the God who holds us fast. There are many courses and strategies to help people find new ways of approaching church. We may be tempted to boost the numbers of our flagging congregations by all kinds of schemes and stunts. We import a success mentality that plays the numbers game. Mysteriously, as we let go of the great missionary quest to bring people in to the church, we at Somewhere Else found that the church has begun to approach us. Sometimes I look at the 20 people sitting around our bread-making table and think to myself, 'I haven't the first idea where you lot came from but I'm very pleased you are here!' God has offered us his church as a gift.

An emerging church like Somewhere Else can be very appealing. It may seem an ideal alternative to a jaded experience of Sunday morning worship. I have, however, a growing sense of appreciation for the tradition from which we spring. It is easy to leap at something new and see it as the new way. Yet there is much wisdom in the old way that should not be lost. 'Holding fast to that which is good' means not throwing the ecclesiological baby out with the postmodern bathwater. When I look at my community I see a truly innovative way of discovering church around baking bread but I also see a strand of being that links us back to the monastic tradition. We have discovered in companionship something of the wonder and depth of friendship that is such a feature of the Society of Friends. Through the bread I have come to a deeper concept of Eucharist that helps me to work with a different understanding of sacrament. Maybe most amazingly, for me anyway, is the discovery that the Somewhere Else community holds fast to much of what the Methodist tradition has valued. We are a small, itinerant community. We believe that the word of God is in the hands of ordinary people. We hold the two strands of scriptural holiness and social action side by side. And most crucially, we are people who experience God's prevenient grace in the ordinary wonderful day-to-day incarnate reality of our community.

So, there are many good things that come to us through the history and wisdom of the Christian church that enrich who we are now. There are also riches that come to us from other places. Our 'code of respect', for instance, is an acknowledged tool of social work settings and counselling. The way in which our kitchen is organized gains wisdom from the catering world. We have learned a great deal on inclusion from our community police officer. 'Holding fast to that which is good' is not simply about claiming the life-giving traditions of the church; it is also about an open ear to much that is good in the policies and ways of relating within those many diverse groups of people around us who are also looking for good practice. If we do this open-heartedly we have nothing to fear. The church doesn't have copyright on goodness.

After five years of eating home-made bread, in a way I have become the bread – or rather the bread has turned into the flesh and blood of me (mostly flesh!). I am often referred to as 'the bread vicar'. There are many ways in which this bread-making thing has formed me. Not only does bread shape our physical form, it also changes our understanding of each other. People say with some pride these days, 'I am a member of the bread church.' We have no doubt that we are a real church and that what is happening with us is good news. This transformation is not simply an outward gesture but rather at the centre of our being. We are in many ways shaped by the bread.

One of the wonders of bread is its power to transform. It transforms our physique, our relationships, our prayers, our community and our city. Bread makes the poor and vulnerable guests of honour at a party. Bread reminds us of those who starve, not as a mind exercise but in our own guts. Bread informs our wilderness experiences and caters for unexpected crowds. Bread takes living things like yeast and turns them into living things like us. Bread gives us life – in all its wonderful and challenging fullness. When Jesus said, 'I am the bread of life', I believe he meant all the above and more besides. Jesus was making a statement not only about his existence but about all existence. Jesus, the bread, is both ordinary presence and extraordinary mystery.

A poem by Heather

Living on the edge
Feeling the sharp edges goudge
Crying out in agony as the grip tightens
Tearing at the guts, pulling up and up
Turning us inside out, red and raw for all
    to see.

Pounding hands and writhing tears an
    outward sign
Of inner pain. Anger shown in spitting
    words and
Grinding teeth, inner torment, spewing
    out.
We fall back exhausted, silent except for
    the sobbing
That continues for ages.

Feeling abandoned on the edge of
    brokenness
There's a ledge, a place to be held,
    supported
A footing, a way of crouching out of the
    bone-chilling wind
Words once snatched away now listened
    to, a story shared

> At the cutting edge, a community, a
> church whose
> Fragility is its strength. Adaptable in its
> uncertainty
> Of existence. Giving out daily bread
> Splintered shards broken and shared.

> No other way to live but on this edge.

Somewhere Else – a story of encouragement?

The story of Somewhere Else is a tale of something that has unfolded when one particular group of people in one particular place began to engage with one particular question. It is not a story from which we can extrapolate a remedy for the whole of the struggle of Western Christianity. Neither is it a permanent solution to the spiritual dilemmas of our postmodern society. It is in essence a very little thing. It is simply a community that is here at the moment and which is trying to be authentic in its engagement with a place and its people.

At another level it is a huge story. It is huge because this small gathering of fragile people has had the courage to face their questions. They have a gospel intention that is a great challenge yet leads to visible transformation. We have seen an excitement and commitment to the gospel imperative that far exceeds this small enterprise.

This is not your story. This is our story. We have to go on working with it. Who knows where we will be in another five years. Your story begins with a different question and will take you to different wonders. All I can say is, have the courage to live your question. It will undoubtedly confuse you. You will face loneliness and bewilderment. You will have to wait and watch beyond your patience and most people will think you are ridiculous. You will be presented with more questions than answers. Undoubtedly you will have to face issues that will challenge you to the core of your being. So have courage. God will come in simple ways. He is ahead of us. He longs for us to live.

From: **Barbara**
To: **Donald**
Date: **17 December 2004**
Subject: **Liverpool Letters**

It seems that when we are suffering most from spiritual agoraphobia then the edges of our open space, which sometimes feel so precipitous, turn into horizons. Through the mists of such personal and theological horizons step the most unlikely people ... through all this there is the need to hold fast and be held in the attention of someone else. To be remembered. Like the city we need to be remembered, and through such calling to mind we are re-made. This becomes the living reality of intercession.

Thank you for remembering us, and for lighting the candles, Donald.

References

Extract from *Alternative Service Book* 1980 is copyright @ The Central Board of Finance 1980, The Archbishops' Council 1999 and is reproduced by permission (4.10.04).

J. Alison, (2003) *On Being Liked*, London, Darton, Longman and Todd

Churches Together in Britain and Ireland (2002) *Time for Action*, London, Church House Publishing

D. Eadie, (1999) *Grain in Winter: Reflections for Saturday People*, Peterborough, Epworth Press

D. Hay, and Rebecca Nye, (1998) *The Spirit of the Child*, Loveland, OH: Fount

R. Ruether, (1983) *Sexism and God Talk*, London, SCM Press

G. Ward, (2000) *Cities of God*, New York, Routledge